Made in the USA
Las Vegas, NV
26 September 2021

The Breath of Cuba

The Breath of Cuba

One Woman's Love Affair
with Cuba's Magic, Music and Men

Part I

By
Cheri Shanti

ISBN: 978-0-99952750-4

Printed in the United States of America.

Book Design by Cheri Lunn.

Contents

Author's Introduction to the Story

I went to Cuba with both a spiritual and a professional mission. The spiritual mission was to gift myself some healing time after a heartbreaking end to an 8 year love affair. The professional mission was to rededicate my life to my path with music, community and culture.

As a drummer in a country that has little of a traditional drum and dance culture of its own outside of what it borrows and takes from the great Rhythm Keepers of the world like Africa; my path with the drum naturally became an eclectic blend of neo-paganism, tribal roots and my own personal expressions. I followed the rhythms wherever they took me. I found myself in a community of musicians, creatives and spirit seekers that ran the gamut from the surreal to the sublime; a community referred to loosely as "*The Pagan Community*." This world became my home for several years. It was here that I got to know my connection with rhythm intimately.

I developed my own unique skills and self-expression. It was a very formative time for my playing as I got to learn and share with both amateur and professional musicians who had expertise with rhythm traditions from around the world. I found myself living in RV's, performing my unique one-woman percussion

show, and traveling across the country following fires and festivals for those first years of my drumming career.

I began being hired to play for all kinds of interesting rituals, ceremonies, workshops and events, with invitations to perform and co-create around the world. I was soon teaching my own programs and making my living entirely through ceremony, drumming, performing and teaching.

For me the drum was, and still is, a metaphor for life. It is a way to connect with the Divine within. Through it I found a connection to God that was intimate and personal, but that also brought me deep into the heart of public community healing rituals.

My first book, *Muse Power: How Recreational Music Making Heals Depression and the Symptoms of Modern Culture,* shares in depth on how drumming and community music rituals can heal and impact both individuals and societies.

As a percussionist, and someone who has worked with music and ceremony for many years; Cuba was, of course, always of great interest to me. Cuba is one of many cultures around the world that uses the magic of rhythm to induce altered states with the intention of bringing about trance and spirit possession for healing purposes.

Santeria ("The Religion," as it is called in Cuba), was of particular interest to me for its combination of drumming, dancing, singing and healing powers.

This kind of a spiritual practice resonates fully with my own spiritual experiences, and with what I feel is the most pure and non-dogmatic form of both personal and community healing.

"La Religion: Santeria"

The Roots of Magic & Music in Cuba

Santeria, commonly referred to as "The Religion", is the primary religion of the Afro-Cubans in Cuba. It is also found on many other Caribbean Islands, in parts of Brazil and South America in different variations. It is a religion proclaimed by practitioners and priests alike for its healing powers. The purest of the Santeria practitioners will insist that it is never to be used for any mal-intent. Santeros in Cuba will go to great lengths to make a point of distinguishing the practice of Santeria from the religions of Voudon, and Palo, which also traveled from Africa so many years ago. Santeros will

often refer to their religion as a "white magic" in direct contrast to the often-misperceived notion of "black magic" that some of the other African Religions are mis-interpreted and labeled as.

The initiation into Santeria requires an intense time of "*Making the Saint.*" In short, this involves a year long process of purification of body, mind and soul. Initiates must dress in only pure white from head to toe, for this entire year. They are required to go through specific ceremonies and divinations to clean them of their past, and open them to receive their highest potential, and most importantly, to heal.

They are to abstain from impurities of thought, mind, body and desire in this time. I have heard countless stories from Santeros from Cuba, about how their lives were transformed through this process, and how more abundance, prosperity, peace and personal power came to them after and during their Initiation.

Santeria has its roots in the Yoruba people of West Africa. When African slaves were brought to Cuba and the Caribbean Islands in colonial times, they were forbidden to practice their African religions freely. In order to survive and avoid harsh punishments, they had to maintain outward appearances of practicing the faith of their Spanish masters.

Similar to the African slaves in other countries, in order to keep their religion and beliefs alive, they syncretized their deities, or *Orishas*, with Christian Saints. In Cuba, it is not uncommon to see statues of Catholic Saints on a Santero's altar, with other representations of the AfricanRoots. There is no confusion in the minds of Santeros. While they know that the Catholic Saints and the Orishas are not identical, they find similarities between them. They see no problem keeping a statue of Saint Barbara, or the Virgin Mary on their altar, as another way of representing their Orishas.

For centuries, Santeria was practiced as a "secret" religion. This was a way to avoid religious persecution and the negative social stigma that was attached to the Afro-Cuban culture in

general. It survived as an oral tradition, passed down from one generation to another, through initiations and ceremonies that created a tightly bound community and distinct lineages based on ancestral connections.

Their Orishas are complex, mystical beings that exist in the wind as *Oya*, the seas as *Yemalla*, the thunder and lightning as *Chango*, in the metals and ores as *Oggun*, and the rivers as *Oshun*, just to name a few. Each Orisha has its own unique attributes, methods, personality and characteristics. Each initiate is aligned with one predominately ruling Orisha as their "*Patron Saint*," that guides their journey on this life. The mythology and stories of the Orishas are told through the rhythms, dances and songs that are integral parts of the ceremonies and rituals performed.

The Religion is indescribably complex. Even the most knowledgeable, wise practitioner will tell you there are many secrets and powers they cannot explain or gain access to. There is a certain mystery around the religion. There is also a very relaxed, casual, family feeling around the ceremonies, as it is very much built into daily family life in Cuba. As a woman and a drummer with a humble curiosity and deeply respectful appreciation of The Religion, I was allowed access to private ceremonies and experiences in Cuba that I know very few non-Cubans will ever get to witness or experience.

I have vowed to keep most of what I was allowed to witness in complete secrecy, in respect to The Religion and to those who permitted me glimpses into this mystical world of magic and music. I am permitted to share with you, however, that what I witnessed was never scary or dark in any way. There were things that were confounding and mysterious, but once the background of situations were explained to me, the healing elements of what transpired made much more sense. Overall, my experience of The Religion was one of family, love, and community. It was an intimate experience of healing through rhythm, trance and community bonding. It was the perfect medicine for my heart, mind, body and soul at the time.

I actually ended up in Cuba more by happenstance than by good planning on the first journey. In the midst of some intense emotional trauma after leaving an 8-year relationship, I met a man named Frank. Frank had big chocolate eyes and a tortured heart, combined with a crazy personality that was almost addictive for me. He was both intensely cynical and wildly comedic. What I liked about him the most, was that he was totally and admittedly transparent, almost to a fault. After spending the last several years with a man whom I had learned to always question and never trust, Frank was irresistible and inviting in his realness. I swore to never be more than friends with this man, knowing he would be an emotional disaster for me. Nonetheless, I was in love with his spirit instantly.

Nearly 6 months after I met him, I was in Costa Rica wrapping up a project on a retreat center that I had helped to bring to life with a dear friend of mine. I caught wind that Frank was going to Cuba via a post on Facebook. I instantly sent him a chat message that just simply said, "I want to come!" Frank said, "Sure," probably thinking I was just talking smack. In less than 24 hours, Frank and I were making plans. Within 48 hours I had purchased my plane ticket. Frank was my portal to Cuba. As it turned out, this was about the extent of our relationship. He left only a few days after I arrived in Cuba, and I have never seen or heard from him again.

Frank's place in my life was purely to open a door for me to the world of Cuba's magic and mystery. A world that I had been secretly desiring to explore for many years. I give great thanks to him for being the person who opened this world to me: a world that continues to inspire and impact my daily life in so many ways.

At this time, my life was transforming rapidly and I was embarking on a journey back to myself. Cuba became my place of refuge, and even more so, my playground, from which to explore new possibilities of what it means to be a human being, and a woman outside of my own cultural norms. I became

obsessed with learning how to dance on the edge of mastery by invoking my primal, intuitive feminine wildness equally with my higher wisdom. This journey led me to changing the name of my business and re-branding my work in the world as a complete lifestyle I named "*The Original Wild and Wise Lifestyle.*™"

My life since then has truly all been an extension of the same process. This lifestyle has become, for me, the supreme journey of self-awareness, self-acceptance, shameless self-expression and self-love. It is my way of connecting authentically to nature, community and the Divine: through myself as myself.

I began to share candidly about my challenges and my healing journey through blogs, and found many women resonating with my sharing. I quickly realized what a great need there is for all of us to be granted full permission and acceptance to be exactly whom and how we are. More importantly, to accept ourselves exactly as we are, and as we are not.

Cuban culture exemplifies these lessons for me in so many ways. While propaganda paints a certain picture of Cubans being dis-empowered and controlled in their expressions (which there is indeed some truth to), what I discovered is that they are actually masters of self-expression. Cuban people have found a myriad of ways to express themselves. They have learned to work around and within a system that challenges them to evolve in ways that are uniquely "Cuban." Through their creativity, their incredible ability to solve any problem by working together, their art, music, boisterous personalities and unique personal styles, Cubans are highly expressed. They have a profound understanding of how to accept the "what is" in life and how to love life despite intensely difficult realities. My personal experience is that Cubans are some of the most expressive, creative and inventive people on the planet. I would also argue some of the most intelligent, loving and straight-forward. They accept each other unquestionably in their own ways of being. They speak their minds unapologetically with each other. This is a big part of what created my passionate

love affair with Cuba. It allowed me to be fully expressed and unapologetically myself in new ways that I have grown to love.

It is also important to mention, as a preface to this book, that this book, and the sequels which will follow, are not written with any particular ideology around politics or religion. The political aspects of Cuba and its impact on Cubans, are a complex web that I do my best to steer clear of. As a non-Cuban, English speaking tourist, and a female, I am granted certain access, privilege and opportunities that are unique. As such, this gives me a very narrow looking glass and the inherent *inability* to truly understand certain aspects of what it might be like to be a Cuban living in Cuba.

My sharings and perspectives are just that: my sharings and perspectives. I do not proclaim to be an expert on The Religion, the history or the politics of Cuba in any way.

This is a book about my personal love affair with Cuba. It touches on many diverse topics and cultural distinctions, but does not subscribe to any one particular ideology or political inclination.

I truly hope you enjoy the journey as much as I have, and I hope you continue to share the journey with me by purchasing the editions that will follow.

This is a Story About Love
Not the kind of love between a man and a woman
Nor the kind of love between a mother and a child
It's not the kind of love that leaves you lost and abandoned
No, not that kind of love that makes you wither and die

But this a story about love
It's the kind of love that makes you reach for the heavens
It's the kind of love that spreads out far and wide
It's the kind of love that knows no boundaries
It's the love that grows from a deep seed inside

It's the love of the self, and the self seen in others
The love of music's way of making us all sisters and brothers
It's the love that transforms and the love that heals
It's the love from within that sweetly reveals

Initiation

There are some things in life that are inexplicable mysteries. There are certain burning passions that make no sense to the rational mind, but that cannot be denied. It is those mysteries which have captivated my heart and may change the course of my life yet again.

A deep, well suppressed calling is screaming now through my skull, penetrating my heart and intoxicating my very being with a desire for its fulfillment. I have left it waiting for so long. Like a cat on the prowl, it has quietly stalked the depths of my soul. I have allowed it to whisper its sweet seductions in the deep heart of night, yet forbidden it access to my waking mind.

I can deny it no longer. It is now an irritable, hungry, awakening creature, coming to life as summer fades into the cold.

This dream is awakening in me now. A dream of granting myself permission to enter another place and time. A dream of allowing the dark, primal pulses of past lives, pure lust and spiritual yearning, to merge in the church of rhythm, spirit and flesh that is my truest sanctuary.

The dream of leaving modernity's maladies of money seeking, soul sucking monotony and re-entering the temple of trance, ceremony and music is alive in me now, more than ever before.

I have no choice but to answer the call.

I am ready.

The Woman
The Wind
&
The Rock

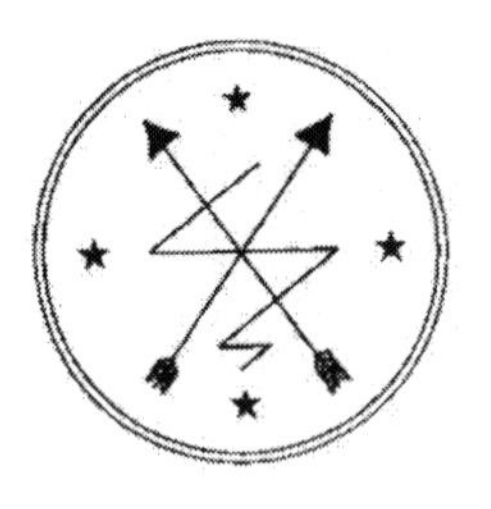

Nothing could feel better than this wind on my skin.

The palm trees are serenading me in wispy waves of sonic sweetness. As my eyelids peel open, I see now the beginnings of this new life. There is no past. At last, I am free. There is no one here that cares or needs to know about it. Quite frankly, nor do I anymore. There is only now, moving into more moments of now, to receive me.

Good wind is better than even the best sex for me. It takes away all pain and offers a resting place in its caress that no man's touch can ever offer. The wind knows every curve of my body, appreciates every hair individually on my head and leaves me satiated to the core of my being: a feat few men can ever dream of coming close to.

The wind here has carried a name since Africans landed on this island hundreds of years ago. It is referred to in the feminine, and she is called "*Oya*." The literal translation from Yoruban is "She Tore." *Oya* is a highly-respected member of a family of deities, commonly known in Santeria as "Orishas" or "Orichas."

Orishas are representations of the Supreme Divinity with roots that come from the deep heart of the Yoruban Culture of Mother Africa. This rock in the Caribbean that I am living on has a thick, deep history and connection with Africa that goes back to the 16th century slave trade. *Oya* traveled here with the Africans, as she did to many of the Caribbean Islands, bringing both solace and death to many throughout the years.

Oya is well known here. Men fear her power and deadly seductions. Wise women smile in acknowledgement of the reflection she offers them of their own true power. She is known as the keeper of the dead, and the guardian of the cemetery. She is the force behind violent storms, lightning, death and rebirth. She is a sumptuous, wild-spirited woman who can be tender, and profoundly sensual, and whom in an instant, can turn into

a raging destructive force, carrying spirits from the other worlds who are at her beck and call.

Oya responds to me, suddenly picking up and blasting me full force as I acknowledge her power over me. She can carry me to the far reaches of this earth and beyond, drop me at will, and leave me breathless with desire for more of her soul stirring, sensual body licking.

It is through her breath that I have heard the songs of the ancestors singing to me from across the seas, beckoning me to this rock. It is she who has been my devoted ally, confidant and guide between the worlds through this life.

Loving the wind is a lucky thing for me. It blows like wild here, sometimes non-stop for days. When she rages, the seas froth and crash against this rock with fury. When she quiets, the gentle lapping of the sea soothes me into stillness. I would take the wind over a man any day, even in her mysterious comings and goings.

The wind never needs coddling, fixing or attention from me to bring its gifts forth. It gives fully with no need for reciprocation or returns.

Ah, sweet Oya, my beloved em-passioned companion. She is always changing, yet her essence remains the same forever more.

She is my eternal lover.

Pandora's Box

I have been in Cuba for less than a month. It feels like a year or more already. Time truly stops here. I saunter down these dusty streets and alleys, carefree and content. No one here looks at me as if I do not belong, even as clear as it must be that I do not. I have never had anyone here so much as raise an eyebrow at me, even as I am cutting through their alleys and backyards, talking to their dogs as if they were my own, in what must sound like garbled Spanish to them. No one seems to notice or care that there is a middle-aged white woman cruising through their village, falling in love with a way of life that many would love to leave behind.

Many people here (but certainly not all) want to travel to the United States or Spain, Italy or anywhere off of this rock. The propaganda of modern culture has impacted some minds to believe that the grass is greener on the other side of the Cuban dilemma.

Many of the Cubans I have met, envision that life for Americans and Europeans is easy, and that being like us will solve all their problems. They envision that all Americans have big fancy houses, cars and easy access to an unlimited supply of money. Some even imagine that life will instantly improve with cell phones and unlimited access to technology. They haven't yet learned the part about how these technologies and devices fry your brain, and distract your artistry. They imagine that more

money is truly the way to more happiness, even if it is at the cost of time spent with your family and friends. Even when it isolates you from your community.

The unfortunate thing about mainstream media and propaganda is that there are too many on both sides of the fence who have bought the whole story: hook, line and sinker. Americans have just as many false illusions fed by the propaganda machine of the USA about life in Cuba, as Cubans have about Americans.

All the truly good things in life that most Americans I know would love to have more of, are already being undervalued here in comparison to "progress" and the "good life" that some Cubans assume all Americans have. I cannot argue that there are certain conveniences and freedoms that are sorely needed here in Cuba. Clearly the people here deserve more opportunities to choose and work towards their preferred lifestyle. Clearly, ease of communication and basic supplies should be more accessible and affordable to all. And there is a great and mounting cost to the rat race of "progress" that is too often shoved under the rug in the never ending race to more, better, faster that we seem to have engaged in. That cost has translated in the United States to some very serious environmental and social issues, including physical and mental health issues, crime, homelessness, violence and sexual deviancy, just to name a very few.

In the United States millions of people are desperately seeking ways to "create community" in a culture that has effectively de-constructed it, right down to the very design of our cities and commercial centers, work places, neighborhoods and institutions. Community has been forced into chat rooms, and onto glowing screens that offer little of true connection and humanity's presence. It is common for people to not know their neighbors, and to live isolated lives, amongst isolated strangers who don't interact or communicate in any way. It is more atypical than typical to find people who actually spend quality time with

their neighbors or their families. Life has become little more than chasing a carrot dangling on a stick.

Depression and disconnection are two of the most commonly reported issues amongst people of all classes, social backgrounds and ages. In an age where we are supposedly more connected than ever, via our gadgets and technology, staggering and ever increasing numbers of people are reporting feeling isolated and alone. The issue is not at all isolated to the United States, although the statistics of the United States lead the way. It has become a global concern of unprecedented proportion. This has increased so much that the Union of International Associates has stated that "*The breakdown of culture and community are the greatest social problems of all time.*"

The Pandora's box of Modernity will eventually find its way to Cuba, as it has the rest of the world. Many Cubans, especially the younger generations, are eagerly and impatiently awaiting that day. However, I learned in my time in Cuba, contrary to popular belief and propaganda, that there are equally as many Cubans who are not so eager for these changes. Many of the elders on the island have witnessed the impacts of modern culture on the people of the world. They know of the social, moral and environmental degradation and problematic issues that have damaged the fabric of humanity and society, in the United States and beyond. They are aware of the crime, the violence, the loneliness, the lack of family and community connections, and the resultant impacts on both the individual and the world. They know and have heard the horror stories of their friends and family members who left Cuba only to find a cold, unwelcoming world where the struggles they faced were equal or sometimes worse than those they faced in Cuba. Many Cubans want absolutely nothing to do with adopting our crazy making, fast paced, race to progress in any way. Striving is not a sport that many of them find a great interest in.

Personally, I stand in the possibility that Cuba can lead the way into an era that finds the balance between progress and

humanity's deeper "*rasion t'etra.*" I like to envision that there will be leaders amongst the young Cubans who will be able to create something never before created on this island. There's a world of curious contemplation for me wondering if they can create something new that can empower, liberate and support people economically and personally, while maintaining the cultural heritage of community, family and organic natural living that makes this island so special.

As these thoughts drift through me, the wind picks up again. A million memories flood my mind and yet I am wrapped in a profound stillness. Three weeks in Cuba doing nothing but writing, singing, dancing and drumming for the pure pleasure of it all has transformed me from the inside out.

My sweet companion Oya is ever present. She brings me home, again and again. I grew up not so far from this rock, so perhaps she knows my name well here.

This is the past too though, and none of that is real anymore. All we ever really have is the moment of Now. It is the still point between the worlds: the one point which encompasses the totality of the past, present and future.

The Now is the only true reality, and how we interact with it has a great effect on the stories we leave behind, as well as the possibilities that we put forth into tomorrow.

Now tells me everything in saying nothing, and nothing in everything. The rational mind can't comprehend any of this, but somehow the soul and spirit are fully, and always in alignment in the Now. For now, I am happy to be here, away from all the drama of the past, away from cell phones, computer screens and the maddening pace of life that modern culture propels me into.

I am in no hurry to return.

I am already fantasizing about how I can disappear here, and stay on this rock in the middle of the sea, making love to the wind every day until I die.

Dreaming Phoenix

The earth stretches out beneath me as my wings expand casting a shadow across the crystal blue sea. I am hungry, but in no rush. The freedom of flight consumes me with bliss.

The soft sweet breeze carries me and I am floating effortlessly on her back. The wind is my ally in the quest for my feast.

Strong talons tucked beneath me, my eyes scan for any movement close to the surface of the sea. I soar from the heights to skim the surface of the sea solely for the joy of it.

I am free, flying effortlessly in full awareness that my hunger will soon be satiated.

Single Woman's Bliss

The wind tickles my bare back lightly and I am startled from a magical space between dreams. With the memory of flying as the Phoenix fresh in my mind, I roll over to feast my eyes on the wind swept sea frothing and spraying next to me.

A wave of joy pulses through me. The phoenix has returned to me again. As always, she leaves me refreshed and invigorated on her return.

My hips love to walk slowly as if they are making love with the earth in every step. This to me is one of the secret magical things about being a woman that I imagine must befuddle the common man.

All I need to do to feel orgasmic bliss is this. A slow walk with the wind licking my skin and I am flowing, with the juices of life dripping out of me.

A man will see me walking in my own bliss and think it is sexy, simply because I am alive, and letting life pulse up from the earth, and down from the heavens into my heart, blossoming thru my chest.

The confusion, for many men it seems, is that they somehow seem to think it is for them and that we, as women, should exist to keep them pleased. (To be fair, I would say almost as many women fall into that story as men.)

A liberated woman in connection with the Divine is a magical, mysterious, and possibly rare phenomenon. Her sensual pleasure may enjoy a man's embrace, but she certainly does not require one for bliss to arise. Sensual bliss is actually her true domain. It is naturally, effortlessly and unquestionably hers.

Union with God can, in fact, be a very sensual and delicious experience in every way imaginable. It takes a true devotion to both solitude and interaction with life to create the unbreakable bond of Divine Awareness of, and with, the Self.

A woman who knows the passion of this divine experience, of union within herself, has little interest in her effect on men sexually. She is not overly concerned with fitting into the societal mold of how and what a woman "should be." She is the pure essence of natural being. Ironically, it is this same woman who will be the most sexually irresistible to men.

An awakened woman is sexy because she derives pleasure and joy from herself, the elements, and life itself. The anatomy of a woman is far more receptive to divine energy flowing inward and in a much more amplified volume than what the anatomy of a male body allows. The channels are naturally much more open. This is just simple physical anatomy. The end result is that a woman can receive, if open, a constant current of energy from her environment. A woman is sexy by nature, not to please a man, but because it feels so damn good to swish the hips and roll in the bliss.

My friend, Ishmael, walks with me often here. I so enjoy our walks together around the small fishing village of Cojimar. In moments, I think he feels what I feel in this way. I think maybe not too many men do. However, I do think in the Caribbean there are more men that understand this than in the United States. The men dance, for one thing, which opens a lot of the energy centers of the body and amplifies their receptivity to life. A man who dances naturally invites more opportunity to tap into the Divine essence of life.

My body is ripe for a lover, and yet I feel too good lately without one to be bothered. I am making love with the Divine again; re-cultivating my own inner sensuality and romance with myself. My love affair with the wind is satisfying me fully for now.

I can now attest that being single at middle age is not really so bad. I am thoroughly enjoying my love affair with the wind on this hot, steamy rock they call Cuba. It is nice to feel delicious, sexy, strong and independent again. I feel liberated, alive and peaceful in a new, more mature, way.

I am free to move on my own flow, to linger when I want to, or not. I am learning to enjoy life again on my own terms. I am most certainly not in any hurry to replace one man with the next. This has never been my way. I have always enjoyed myself in life with or without a man by my side.

I may be a rare breed, but the truth is that I do not in any way believe that having or finding a partner is the primary objective or entire reason for my existence. Even as a young girl, the whole idea of getting married and "settling down," just never felt like the driving force of my life the way it seemed to be for many other women I have known. I have always seen the times in between relationships as being my most powerful periods of self-growth and creativity, connecting me more to Divinity in all of its forms, expressions and opportunities.

I have never understood how people can relationship hop, one to the next, without giving themselves some time alone. To each their own, but I would rather give myself some time to heal and reconnect my own internal dots, before jumping into what would likely just be a re-run anyway. I love myself and truly enjoy having time to indulge in the worlds of my own creation.

If I truly wanted a lover, one is never hard to find. Finding willing companions for any woman with her wits about her, is never a difficult task. There is no difference here on this rock. There are so many beautiful men here, and just about any of them would willingly be available at a moment's notice for a playful romp in the sack. Sexy, strong-bodied, steamy, lustful men with

skin stretched over perfectly sculpted muscles are plentiful. Their desirous eyes consume me as I walk by. I am learning to enjoy these brief, passionate moments of connection we share.

Cuban men are undoubtedly some of the hottest men I have ever seen in all my travels around the world. They emanate a stimulating, innate confidence matched with a tender hearted innocence and a deeply primal, provocative, sexual energy that is distinct from any other culture's masculine expression.

Cuban men can be just straight up, jaw-dropping hot, and it's more than just physical. It's a sexiness that comes from the inside out. I know many of them are likely married or in relationships. I also know that most of them probably have a host of other women they enjoy from time to time. It's just a part of the culture here and for the most part it is accepted and not at all frowned upon.

For the self-righteous women out there, who want to scorn the brothers, don't get on your high horse too fast. Many of the women are equally as promiscuous as their male counterparts in Cuba, and more secretive. It is very much an accepted cultural norm, with roots that go back to Mama Africa's ways. Even if it's not spoken, it's understood. In a culture that is as loving and sensually alive as Cuba, it's worthy of consideration to give up on all of your prudish and monogamous concepts of how love can or should be.

One thing I find that Cuba shares with the rest of the world is that most men are a bit clueless on how to treat a woman with the kind of respect and care she requires to blossom fully into her most receptive, powerful Queendom. Yet, in truth, both men and women are too often programmed incorrectly in this world. Too few of us know how to truly honor and respect each other's differences, without domination, control or manipulation. This ignorance serves only to perpetuate a sad state of confusion between men and women around the world.

In a healthy balanced dynamic, an awakened sensitized man is pleased most by pleasing, supporting and providing security

and strength to a woman. She, with or without him, is alive and sensually awakened simply by the touch of the wind on her skin. She is in turn honored to be there to support, empower and be the calm, clear space of divine guidance that he needs to become an empowered force of masculinity, initiative and focalized power in the world.

If it means another three year-round of celibacy to wait for a lover worthy of this love, a lover who truly gets this way of being together, then so be it. I will wait and enjoy the journey fully until then. The wind is serving me well enough.

Cuba Captured
Global Citizen

I'm a simple woman really,
but not so easily coerced into domesticity.

The culture I was born into
is not the truth of my heart and soul.

I am called to explore all of myself in this life.

I recognize that I am no longer a resident
of one small town in the United States.

I am a being that can find home anywhere I go.

I am a Cuba Captured, Global Citizen.

The colors on this island are vibrant and decaying. The salt air and wind, combined with years of neglect from a lack of resources, have created a starkly beautiful and surreal landscape here. It touches on some nostalgic quality of life the way the colors fade into their own death, beaten down by wind, water and sun. Black bodies silhouetted against tapestries of vibrant decay make for images that stick to the mind's eye throughout eternity.

I have experienced some beautiful places on this earth and loved a lot of people around the world. Cuba however, has captured me, body, mind, heart and soul, in a way I never knew possible. There is something in the quality of the energy here that is raw and so intrinsically primal. Cuba has an energy that is so sensual, so sexual, so alive and hungry for life, that it sings to a place in my soul that has never before been serenaded.

And yet, even in my fantasies of staying here, of disappearing from the modern world and quietly sinking into the fabric of a simple island life, I am all too aware of the very real challenges of a life in Cuba. It is not always easy to acquire even the most basic of items. Simple products that we take for granted in the United States, like dish soap, toothpaste, shampoo, or toilet paper for example, can sometimes be very hard to come by. Eggs, milk, fresh fruits and vegetables are sometimes readily available, and sometimes not so readily available.

It is not uncommon to see empty shelves in the small groceries that do exist. As a foreigner, there are many days I pray I can find enough bottled water to drink, as it seems the few stores in Cojimar are always running out. Being here only a few weeks, I am not really willing to risk trying the tap water, although I have boiled water more than once when I could not purchase any at the store.

Communication on or off island can be completely impossible some days. There are very few cell phones on the island at present[1],

1 2010.

and phone calls both on and off island are very costly. Internet is not only painfully slow, but also very expensive.

At the hotels in Cojimar and Havana, where there are a few, very slow, archaic computers available for tourists to use, the price is almost $9 an hour[2]. It can take nearly a whole hour to get one email to go through some days. Most days I just can't be bothered to waste my time or money sitting there watching the dial spin. I find it infuriating even at normal speeds in the USA, so watching it spin for an hour is worse than watching paint dry on a rainy day.

The people, by Western standards, live very humbly. They simply do not have the kind of material abundance that we have in the United States, and yet no one is starving or without a place to live. Homelessness and starvation are almost completely non-existent in Cuba[3]. Everyone is fed, housed and somehow taken care of.

Most Cubans I've met are well educated, strong and healthy, since education and healthcare are basic human rights for Cuban Nationals. Plenty of people here are plump and round enough to be considered overweight. This, of course, may speak equally to the poor quality of food, as much as an over indulgence in the consumption of the most common foods. Pizza, bread, refined sugar and white rice are not the healthiest foods, but they are by far the most consumed, plentiful and affordable. Fresh vegetables and produce are often out of reach on the average Cuban salary, and again, they can often be hard to come by.

The financial game in Cuba is a complexity unlike any in the world. Making enough money here to live well is difficult by

---

2 2010 Price in Cuba for Internet.

3 2010: I noticed on later trips in 2016 there were a few homeless people in the cities. Housing prices in certain tourist areas were forcing some Cubans out as foreigners and travelers were taking more spaces for tourism and commerce. In some places, Cubans going from one small town to a bigger city to work could not afford the rental rates in the city they came to work in. I met several sleeping in the parks and streets, who were looking to find something they could afford on their low wages.

design. The government takes a pretty good cut of any income produced, and as of now[4], owning one's own business is very difficult for a Cuban National. Owning a car is completely out of reach of the average Cuban. Walking, biking, horses, public transport and taxis are the primary ways of getting around.

However, what the people are lacking in money and material resource, is made up for in what they have in family, community and friendships. There is an incredible wealth of a much more human kind in Cuba; a richness beyond any form of material wealth imaginable. It exists in the simple sharing of humanity. It is this immeasurable wealth that is an intangible infinite source of life, well-being and sustenance for Cubans. I believe it is a way of being that we in the modern world, would be wise to consider re-learning to assist us in the healing of our hearts, minds and societies on planet Earth.

Here in Cojimar, during the night, the streets are lit up with life until the wee hours. Practically every porch hosts groups of people talking and sitting in their government-distributed, wooden, carved rocking chairs. In a very few homes, the glow of a TV can be seen, but even then, the sounds you hear are of people talking, laughing and enjoying their time together. Most of what is shown on the television are re-runs and tightly controlled government propaganda that they have seen over and over, yet they still chat over it and talk about it each time like it's the first time they have ever seen it.

It is common and typical for Cubans to stay up well past midnight, just casually shooting the shit, sometimes playing dominoes, or singing songs, drinking rum or coffee, sharing food and enjoying their humble homes together. As neighbors pass by, they will shout out at their friends as they walk by, "Hacere! Que Bola?" This is a distinctly Cuban greeting which translates

4 At the time The Breath of Cuba Part I was written, Cubans still could not own their own businesses. There have been many changes since then, but still many challenging factors for the average Cuban to face around economics.

basically into "What's happening?" "How's it going?" or "What's up?"

Cubans commonly refer to each other as "mi familia" or my family, even when there is no blood relationship. Everyone is "Hermana" or "hermano" (sister or brother), "mami" or "papi" (mom or pop), "sobrino" or "nina" (nephew or daughter). They welcome outsiders in the same way they do their own family, with food, coffee, rum, and joyful celebratory sharings. Cubans are masters of the art of conversation. They openly discuss their problems, concerns and lives together. They are always willing to help each other through any issue, no matter how complex or challenging. They will spend hours in conversation to explore every possible angle of creating a solution.

Companionship, community and sharing are at the very core of this culture. They will always invite you in to sit and share whatever they have with you, even if what they have is very little. Cuban people have a natural sense of comfort and connection with each other, and with humanity in general. I find it to be super rich, nurturing and incredibly transformative in contrast to the culture I was raised in.

Mind you, I didn't have a bad or deeply traumatic upbringing by any means. I had a good family and a somewhat story book life by outward appearances. My parents never divorced. There were no obvious or big issues with crime or deviancy in my neighborhood. I dealt with pretty normal high-school dramas of that time. We certainly did not have high school shootings back then and for that I am deeply grateful. We did however have a few race riots with sticks, knives and baseball bats, that were the predecessors to the gun violence of today.

I grew up in a safe and quiet small town in South Florida where nothing much really happened. While growing up, I sort of knew my neighbors. We waved when we drove past them on the street, and they knew my name, and I theirs.

That was about the extent of it. I might have entered one or two of their homes as a child, but only really in the foyer or

maybe the back porch. I would say it was an average normal upbringing for a middle-classed American at the time, in the 70's and 80's. Neighbors were the people who lived around you, but certainly not people you really connected with beyond basic cordiality. They were basically still strangers, people I was mostly taught to keep at arm's length rather than truly sharing life or connecting with.

The painful, but honest truth is that even my own family felt like strangers to me. There was a distance, a coolness, and an unspoken tension that was always present, even in the extended family. That distance always befuddled me. It was the source of a deep loneliness and sense of isolation in the world for me. What seemed so normal and acceptable to everyone else around me, was completely perplexing to me at a very young age. Most people I knew had similar dynamics in their families and communities, and so it quickly became normalized for me.

I knew deep inside however, that there was another way, and so the quest for the relaxed enjoyment of sharing in the human experience has become one of the primary driving forces in my life. In my commitment to breaking down my cultural and familial conditioning, I have delved into the heart of what it means to be a human being. I have questioned the norms, ways and means that my culture has indoctrinated me into. I have actively sought out individuals, cultures, communities and teachings that have helped me to become a *more human* human being.

My culture tried to teach me to fear the other, and that strangers could not be trusted. It tried to convince me that there were enemies amongst us, and that family was only about your blood relations. It taught me that talking to strangers was a really bad and dangerous idea. Eventually, over the years, my culture's controllers replaced the need to talk to anyone with technology.

Today, if I need directions to get somewhere, my gadget tells me where to go. There is no need to stop and talk to anyone anymore. My gadget never stops beeping, buzzing and vibrating.

If I didn't set boundaries around it, I would never have time to meet or talk with anyone in person anymore.

When I need to buy gas or purchase products, I do not even have to get out of my car or leave my home. If I wanted to, I could just swipe or enter numbers from a plastic card and have no interaction at all with anyone and have anything and everything I want delivered to my front door.

The media blasts me daily with images and stories of shootings and random acts of senseless violence, sending a strong message that it is not safe anywhere: not in an airport, not in a school, not in a grocery store, not in a mall, and most certainly not in the streets at night. We are told to lock your doors, and keep to yourself. Even those you think are your friends, could be out to get you. Trust no one. Mind your own business.

This of course isn't literal and direct, but there is a tremendous amount of fear propaganda that we are exposed to from mainstream media, on a daily basis. Most people have stopped noticing or questioning this ever present backdrop to our reality in the US. Even fewer seem to really understand the long-term impact of this kind of cultural conditioning. Thankfully, there is a counter culture also that knows, as I do, that we can create something else by sharing good will and learning to break down those barriers within ourselves, our communities and our families.

What Cuba offers to me is a distinct polar opposite of everything the mainstream component of my culture has offered me. The healing I have experienced as a result of the love, family vibes and open hearted generosity on this island will influence and impact me for the rest of my life.

I am indeed Cuba Captured. I know that my life will never be quite the same again. Even with all of its challenges, my dream of returning to this beautiful Rock in the Caribbean to learn more from this "familia de me Corazon" (family of my heart) remains strong and unmoved. As the winds blow, so shall I go and return again in perfect time.

The Dream

Again he finds me here.

My racing heart stops and I fall into him.

Always elusive, he intrigues my senses
and demands my full awareness.

I can not resist his dark, powerful presence.

I surrender fully to the weakness of my desire.
He holds me and we are stillness in motion.

His lips find mine.

In a flash it is dawn emerging.

I go to the sea to greet the dawn.

Rhythm Hunter

My mind is still. I am still contemplating the passionate dream that just woke me, of the lover I do not yet know. His face is still a mystery. He visits me in my dreams on occasion. He is dark, sensual, and always holds my face in his perfectly sculpted hands. I rarely think of these dreams more than a moment after I rise, but today the desire lingers.

The dawn is cool, sweet and refreshing to my spirit. The wind, as always, loves every part of me and carries my mind to timelessness: past, present and future are all one.

There is no me. I am the wind. I am the sea here beneath these rocks, tasting the shore. I am the sun rising as the moon sinks behind the horizon in the western sky. I am home. Nothing can touch me, like nothing can capture the wind. I am free and uncontainable. I am unstoppable. I can slip through or blow over any obstacle. I am timeless, eternal and unscathed by any man. I am the all of life and death. I am one with this earth, as I am with the stars and sky.

Through Oya's breath, I hear the drums again. The sound brings me back into this 5'3 form that timelessness is choosing to play within now. My still-awakening consciousness works to convince me that the drums are only there in my mind. They seem so close. If only I could find them.

My mind speaks rational thought: it is 7:00 a.m. No one is playing drums right now. The rhythms always sing to me in the wind. They find me through Oya's whispers and seductions. They have lived in me for lifetimes beyond this one, and now, being here on this island, it seems they haunt me incessantly. They are always elusive, coming from across the sea, or far down an alleyway.

I sometimes spend an afternoon following them for hours, and usually I find nothing. They seem to be always just out of my reach, yet they are with me, always intoxicating me here night and day.

Cuba's drumming traditions are a whole world and lifetime of study in and of themselves. A casual, uninformed observer witnessing a group of drummers in the midst of a Bembe[5] or other religious ceremony in Cuba, may think it is just another form of entertainment, and can unintentionally insult or offend the Cubans, and their religion. Taking photos, for example, or walking in front of a dancer or drummer in trance, can be seen as blatant signs of ignorance, and disrespect.

A bembé is a party for the Orishas in the Santeria Religion. During a bembe the Orishas are praised, saluted and invited to join the party through a 'mounting' of one of the practitioners. Through songs, rhythms, and movements that have been used for thousands of years, the Orishas are called forth to bring their gifts of divinity, healing and transformation from the Spirit world to the realm of the physical.

The rhythms are critical to the success of the ceremony. Drummers practice assiduously for years to be able to play these intricate rhythms with precision and accuracy. Since the drums are "speaking" to the Orishas, they are tuned in such a way as to play the tones of Yoruba speech. For this reason, some rhythms are never played unless it is in religious context, as it is believed it could offend the Orisha it is meant to honor. The rhythms are actually prayers to the deities. Each Orisha has its own rhythms, songs and dance.

While not all drumming has a specific religious intent in Cuba, the roots of most of the drumming traditions come from the heart of the African religions, the most commonly known in Cuba being Santeria. When played in religious contexts, each rhythm is its own world, its own invocation of spirit, and its own time capsule, that tells its own unique story. The dances are embodiments of stories told through hundreds and sometimes thousands of years, with particular movements signifying

5 Bembe: A religious ceremony of Santeria using drums, dance and song to invoke the Orishas.

particular aspects of the stories, and particular characters who represent Divine expressions of the Godhead.

As a drummer and lover of all things rhythmical, it is only natural that I find myself on this rock in the Caribbean making love to the wind and chasing rhythms through her breath all day and night.

And yet, traditionally, I am forbidden to play many of them here. As a woman, the tradition is not meant for me. It is a belief on the island that is slow to change. It is a commonly held belief amongst male drummers that the drums lose their power when a woman plays, and that a woman can lose her vitality by playing.

I, of course, have experienced quite a different reality being a woman who has played professionally for many years with intense power and passion. I will not and do not argue with them here. I treat it all with complete respect and mindful consideration.[6] In Havana this is starting to change, but even there, the density of resistance to female drummers is thick.

The Bata drum for example, is traditionally not to be played by women. The belief that was shared with me by my teachers in Cojimar, is that because the drum is held across the legs in front of the abdomen, it puts stress on a woman's reproductive organs and can affect her ability to bear children. Since women's primary role is to bring forth children, it is for her protection, and the protection of life itself, that she is forbidden to play.

The Bata drum is a double-headed drum shaped like an hourglass with one end larger than the other. It is used primarily for religious purposes. Three bata of varying sizes are played together to create intricate poly-rhythms that carry practitioners and dancers into deep states of trance.

---

6 As a woman from the U.S. and because of the special connections I had with my teachers, I was granted certain non-gender specific privileges to experience things that I know are not customary or traditional. I was allowed to play Bata and to bear witness to ceremonies that are not typically open to outsiders. These are parts of my story I gave my word to maintain in the utmost privacy out of my respect for the deep secret worlds of Santeria.

The drum came from the land of Yoruba, located in Nigeria. It is now commonly used in the practice of Santeria and also in non-religious applications such as jazz and more esoteric combos. Bata dates back over 500 years, and is believed to have been introduced by a Yoruba king named Shangó el Rey Del Tambor. It was the 1800's slave trade that brought awareness to the instrument with over 300,000 Africans who were brought to Cuba at that time.

And of course, there is the fascinating and secret society of the Abakuá which is only for men. Abakuá is an Afro-Cuban men's initiatory secret society which originated from south-eastern Nigeria, and southwestern Cameroon. It was believed that Ńáñigos, as the members are known, could be transformed into leopards to stalk their enemies. In Africa, they were notorious operators who made regular deals for profit with slavers.

The rhythmic dance music of the Abakua combined with Bantu traditions of the Congo contributed to the musical tradition of Rhumba. Even more interesting, an analysis of Cuban popular music recorded from the 1920's until the present, reveals Abakuá influence in nearly every genre of Cuban popular music.

This demonstrates the influence of the religions on the popular culture of Cuba. The music of the Abakuá is played with four drums: three playing the melody and one playing lead or improvising with the dancer and songs. This is similar to Rhumba which takes the secret world of the Abakuá to the streets for a sexy, sensual dance that invites the community to play.

Traditionally performed by poor workers of African descent in streets and "solares"(courtyards), Rhumba remains one of Cuba's most characteristic, loved and well known forms of music and dance. It is a dance enjoyed by all people, of all ages, just about everywhere in Cuba. The music and dance are non-religious and purely social in nature. Rhumba is the music to bring people of all ages and backgrounds together purely for enjoyment and pleasure.

I love Rhumba for its provocative sensuality and its honoring of both genders for their strengths and enjoyment. It so beautifully and playfully displays the courtship of a man for a woman. It accents her flirtatiousness and his persistence, through a fun and delightful journey of song, dance and drumming.

It does not escape me that there are hundreds of rhythms and dances to learn about in Cuba. A lifetime of study is available here on this ragged rock. There are complex strings of historical occurrences and a myriad of cultural influences that have impacted Cuba's musical sensibility over time.

I am well aware that I am just barely sniffing around the edges exploring into a world of music, spirit and magic that goes back thousands of years to ancient Africa. The songs and calls I hear through Oya's Breath are incantations of a million souls dancing between the worlds. They are whispering into my slumbering soul to wake me up. I willingly listen to the stories they have to share with me.

I am honored to have been allowed to hear and heed the call, even if just for a short time. I could die here right now and be quite content. The wind, my beloved, timeless lover, holds me sweetly between the worlds and could carry me through the void with ease. I have waited too long to be here now to die today though, so I rise from my seaside perch and walk to Ishmael's house, cutting thru backyards and chatting with everyone I meet along the way.

Finding Family

La Familia de Corazon

Ishmael

A smiling giant pops through the door today speaking perfect English, "Cheri, Hello. How are you?" I almost have a smile attack. My beloved angel and brother, Ishmael is visiting me first thing in the morning, speaking his first greeting to me in English so beautifully. He came so we could walk together this morning to town to get food for his chickens. Our days here are coming to a close and we are both saddened by that reality. I always enjoy our walks together. We laugh so much. The easy graceful presence we share together is so pure, like true brother and sister.

Every day we are more in love, as we learn how to communicate thru the language barrier. Not too long after our walk, when I returned to his home after breakfast, I found him sitting in his house with big tears rolling down his beautiful black face. In one hand he held a photo, faded and tattered, the other hand framed his face. I put my hand on his shoulder to comfort him but said nothing.

I knew my silent presence was enough. "Mi hermano: hoy es el aniversario de su muerte." He was mourning the loss of his brother who had died on this day some years ago. I embrace him softly, as his tears fall. We light a candle together and send prayers to his brother in the spirit world. Later, I returned with sweets to place on his brother's altar. He hugs me hard in gratitude for

this simple gesture. Touched, I left him in his mourning with a tender heart and a gentle smile.

Ishmael is a true angel. I am quite sure he has been sent from the Gods, to protect and guide this journey for me. He is a giant of a man, towering at 6'3. He is soft but very strong. It is clear that his size, stature and presence command a certain respect in Cojimar from the way he is greeted and treated by those who stop in to visit. It is his presence that anchors me here in this dusty little village, with his kindness and big loving heart. Ishmael is my place, and person, of refuge and friendship. He is the big brother I never had, but always wanted, always caring for me in such a sweet and special way. I would trust this gentle giant with my life, and often it feels that I have.

It is a complete relief and gift to have such a beautiful strong male ally here, one who is not trying to get into my pants or seduce me into marriage. He is elegant, refined and articulate, with no sexual overtones at all. We are learning to communicate pretty well, despite the language barrier. However, I am certain at least half of what he tells me I misinterpret or do not fully understand, and probably vice versa.

The lack of any sexual or personal agenda other than companionship, allows us access to being silly and free together like children. His spirit, at 48, is so pure and so precious to me. When it comes out to play, I am continuously moved into deeper love. We laugh together and sometimes we cry together at the state of the world. We talk about everything from politics to personal tragedies. His smile lights up my world here every day!

I picked Ishmael out of a sea of swarming bodies or perhaps, I was divinely guided to him somehow. Frank and I were walking through town the night I arrived in Cojimar. On our way, we met a Cuban American man who was visiting family there in Cojimar. He just happened to be a resident of my brother's home town in Florida. When he inquired about my trip, I shared with him that my intention was to learn more about Santeria, the

Orishas and Bembe. He excitedly told me that there was a Bembe happening “right now” very close to his father’s home.

“All the people there are dressed in white. You can walk there now and see. I don’t know so much about it, but you can go and see if it’s still going.” I was grateful he spoke English in that moment and wasted no time. I thanked the messenger and he continued on his way.

Excited, I grabbed Frank’s arm and half dragged him down the street. “I don’t know if we should go there. Maybe they’ll try to sacrifice us,” he said in his witty, sarcastic way, with a devious, but scared smile on his face. I knew he was joking. I also knew that he had some real fear brewing. The closer we got to the house, the more his anxiety increased.

“Don’t worry Frank, I’ll protect you.” I laughed as I said it. “We are safe, trust me.” I said, with total confidence. The truth was, I had absolutely no idea what to expect and no idea whatsoever if it was a good idea to show up there unannounced, or if it would be considered inappropriate. After all, I had been in Cuba less than 8 hours. I knew absolutely nothing. I had never been to a Bembe of any kind. I had no idea what the protocol was for a stranger; particularly a woman from the United States. I had not even figured out yet if I was considered friend or foe to the Cubans on the island.

Somehow though, in my heart, I just knew it was OK. I knew that I was being divinely guided and that we were safe. I could feel that magic was on my side this night as the wind kicked up a notch and the clouds parted to let the moon shine down on us.

When we arrived at the house, the music had just stopped and people started spilling out into the street chatting, laughing and congregating in small groups.

“Oh well, it’s over, let’s go,” Frank said turning away, trying to make a fast break.

"No, no. We wait. I want to talk to someone and ask some questions," I said. I stood my ground, holding onto his arm and pulling him close, keeping him there with me.

He was visibly uncomfortable, "Let's go, I don't think it's a good idea. Can't we come back in the morning?" He whined, practically shaking with anxiety and discomfort.

I could not help but laugh at this grown man so afraid of these beautiful people who had just been praying together. I stood my ground. "No, no, just wait. I'm looking for the right person to talk to." I said.

His sarcasm kicked in again, "And how are you going to know, will he be carrying a sign that says, 'American girl: just ask me'?"

I laughed, and couldn't really answer him. I just knew that I would know and trusted in my intuition. At that instant, my eyes landed on the man I knew I needed to talk to. He was the tallest, biggest man in the street, towering over everyone else. He had an undeniable strength and a refined quality of dignified elegance about him. It was clear that he was a respected man in the community by the way people responded to him and acknowledged him as he walked past them. His laughter and good natured spirit poured out of him effortlessly. He walked with two women, one on either side of him. The way he moved spoke of an inner power, a Divine presence that was unmistakable. I sensed a profound gentleness that even his enormous size couldn't hide.

"Come on," I said to Frank and we followed him down the street. Frank never stopped trying to talk me out of approaching him, and when I could not bear to listen to his nonsense another moment, I finally left him behind and caught up with this big Cuban man and his two escorts.

I called out to him in my broken Spanish from behind him, "Disculpme, senor?"

He stopped and turned to look at me with a blank stare. I did not give myself time to think about what I would say, I just

jumped in with both feet. The insecurity of my poor grasp of his language gave way to my conviction to connect.

"Me llama Cheri, y yo se no conoces me, pero, estoy aqui para apprender que puedo de Santeria. No se si esta bien para me preguntarte ahora, pero, puedes ayudarme encontrar los personas correcta?" (My name is Cheri, and I know you don't know me, but I am here to learn what I can about Santeria. I don't know if it's ok for me to be asking you right now, but can you help me find the right people?")

In my pathetic Spanish, I attempted to first apologize for not knowing if this was a respectful and appropriate time to talk to him, and for not yet understanding the culture or customs. I told him I had just arrived on the island a few hours ago. I did my best to explain to him my intention and reason for talking to him. In the best way I could, I shared with him my desire to study the drum and the religion to learn whatever I was allowed to learn in their customs and traditions. I must have sounded ridiculous in my babble.

For a few moments, I was afraid I had made a mistake. He looked down at me with a blank look on his face, which could have meant just about anything. I was not sure if he was going to yell at me for being so ignorant or laugh at me. In fact, I was not even sure if he understood what I had just attempted to say.

I could see Frank out of the corner of my eye fidgeting and backing away like a scared child. I just stood there with my hand on my heart in humble grace, my eyes fearlessly loving, watching this big black giant of a man stare back at me.

It was a long pregnant pause with us locked into each other's eyes as if he was making an assessment of my soul, and looking deep beyond my form. I felt our connection in ways that are not from this time, and for a brief moment there was a tangible stillness between us. Without changing expressions, he dryly said, "Benga," and turned, walking ahead of me with the two women, talking to them as if I did not even exist. I had no idea where I was following him to, or what was happening, but I had

all green light good vibes inside from head to toe. I followed along, with Frank grabbing my arm whining to me, "Let's go, come on, they're going to sacrifice us now, I just know it."

I laughed and felt giddy inside, put my finger to his lips and said, "Sh, how do you know if they speak English or not, don't be ridiculous. Come on."

"I know, I know. I'm just kidding," he said and yet inside I knew he was a little anxious and maybe a little concerned for me. It's well known that many foreigners get taken advantage of in Cuba and worked over for hundreds and sometimes thousands of dollars under the guise of The Religion. I could feel his genuine concern for me, and I appreciated that I had someone with me to watch my back if needed.

I was smiling ear to ear inside. My first night in Cuba and already the magic was unfolding. It was a very good sign, and just as I felt that smile come into my heart, the wind kicked up a notch and blew through my hair. Ishmael and the women lifted their heads in front of me. He turned and looked at me for a moment, studying me with a keen curiosity written across his brow. I just bowed my head in gratitude.

"Me nombre es Ishmael," he said and the hint of a smile crossed his face before he turned back to his companions again.

I walked behind him, with Frank falling behind me a few steps. We walked a few blocks to a big white gate. "Ven Aca," he said, motioning to me. I entered the gate into the house.

"I'll wait here," Frank said cowering on the street outside nervously. I followed the three Cubans in front of me and entered a house filled with black bodies all dressed in pure white from head to toe.

My first few hours in Cuba and I had no idea whether I had made a mistake, or not. I didn't know whether my courage was being commended or mocked, yet I felt no fear. What I felt was a striking, surreal and overwhelming feeling of family. The only discomfort I felt was in not knowing the language. Even still, I felt comforted and like I belonged there, like it was the most

normal thing in the world for me to be there. No one seemed to really notice me much, and I didn't get any kind of special treatment or recognition. They all just went on chatting and laughing.

My first initiation was having the courage to follow my heart and speak to this giant of a man, and then having the courage to step past that gate.

Ishmael returned from the back of the house and found me on the porch, "Regresses manaña a las diez en la manaña," he said to me and then he subtly, but clearly, dismissed me. I had no idea what I was coming back for, but I knew I would be there and on time. My first night there and I had found what would be my first true friend, guide, and opening to the family of The Religion of Santeria.

I found Frank waiting for me practically chewing his nails off out front. Together we made the trek back to the guest house where we were staying, about 15 minutes away from the house of Ishmael.

I laid myself down to sleep that night feeling so full, so blessed and so perfectly welcomed to the island of Cuba on my first day.

I was excited to discover what Day 2 would be like.

The Jesus's

I arrived the next morning at 10:00 a.m. sharp. Ishmael welcomed me with a huge ear to ear smile. He showed me in to his home, motioning for me to sit. He spoke non-stop in fast Cuban Spanish. I pretended I understood what he said and sat down quietly while he poured coffee for me.

I realized I really had no clue what he was saying to me, but I did my very best to listen intently to get any clues on what he was saying that might help me to gain some clarity on what this first meeting was all about today. He was jovial, loud and filled with life, chattering a mile a minute.

His couch was covered in an old sheet with the stuffing from inside popping out of the sides, the upholstery a faded memory, worn through completely from too many years of wear. I noticed his altar immediately in the corner under an image of him with his eyes popping out, bent in half, holding onto his ankles, wearing all white.

He noticed my gaze and rambled off on a tangent in Spanish. I know I missed a lot but I was able to understand that he had been an actor for many years in the theater in Havana. I felt some sadness in him around the story he told. I got that there had been a conflict of some sort, maybe with his boss or the director of a show, that had closed the door for him to his world in theater. I hoped that someday I would get a glimpse into understanding more of what he was sharing with me.

This was only the second Cuban home I had been in, and so I was taking it all in. The smells, the energy, and the reality of how my new friend lived, day to day, was unfolding already before my eyes. The house was clean, simple and in desperate need of care and attention. Huge cracks ran up the concrete walls and into the ceiling. The paint was chipping and peeling everywhere. The ceiling was flaking off in large crusty pieces of paint and cement. The unmistakable smell of mold was heavy and strong in the air. There was a mid-sized antique of a TV in front of the tattered couch, a love seat and some iron backed chairs with thin splintering pieces of plywood as the seats, a small table with a lamp and a fan in the living room, and nothing more. I could see he had the bathroom door closed and that the bathroom door was falling off, in need of repair.

I shared my story with him the best that I could in Spanish. He seemed to understand most of what I was saying, which was at least somewhat encouraging on my second day in Cuba. Through our first real conversation, I was able to understand enough to comprehend that he had arranged for me to start taking drum lessons there at his home with his neighbor, whose name seemed to be Jesus.

For the teachings of the religion, Ishmael would be my guide and answer any questions I had. For the music and drumming, Jesus would be my teacher. He then led me through the kitchen that stunk of rotting meat and dairy, out to the back of the house, into an open-air courtyard.

There, on a raised concrete step, beneath a tin roof, sat two drums and four iron chairs with no backs, and wood planks for seats. This was to be my classroom for the next 3 weeks. I smiled inside at the simplicity and the very real cultural context I would learn in. It was perfect.

The courtyard smelled strong of animal feces and rotting flesh. It was flanked on all sides by cages. Ishmael walked me around the courtyard to visit his animals which consisted of two enormous pigs, chickens and some random cats and dogs that

lolly-gagged around. He explained to me that this was his work: he raised animals for sale. His enthusiasm and excitement about sharing this showed his love for the very animals he knew he would eventually lead to slaughter.

A few moments later, a tall, skinny black man walked around from the side of the house smoking a cigarette. He had piercing eyes that looked right through me. He cordially kissed my cheek as is the customary greeting in Cuba. He then took my hands in his, turned them over and studied them. "Tu tocas?" He asked me in disbelief. Then, without waiting for a response, he sat down at the drum and gave me a rhythm. I smiled, sat down and matched him perfectly. We played freely in an opening exploration of each other. I followed his lead and humbly let him explore with me. As a drum teacher myself, I intuitively recognized that he was sizing me up to know how, and where, to start with me. I was also doing the same with him. We both felt the mastery of the other and connected in the world of rhythm as kindred souls.

"Ok, Ok, Ok," he said and laughed out loud, clearly pleased and smiling. "Wow," he said to me, shaking his head softly. He excitedly spoke to Ishmael, and they exchanged laughter and a seemingly deep conversation for about 5 minutes that was totally incomprehensible to me. I didn't catch a word of it, but the energy was high and definitely entertaining.

Jesus's Spanish was impossible for me to grasp, it was so open and round. There were sounds coming from him I had never heard before. I wondered how it would be to study with him, but I was just too happy to care in that moment. Seeing him smiling and happy was all I needed to understand.

Ishmael stood behind me. They both laughed heartily, commenting in Spanish about my playing with excitement and surprise in their voices. A few neighbors had gathered at the gate behind us while we were playing. They were also chatting with a sense of curiosity and approval. I laughed imagining their thoughts. Out of nowhere, a skinny little white woman shows up in their quiet, little village, playing drums like a wild child

with one of the top master drummers in the village, and they had front row seats for the premier debut.

I laughed with them, and humbly bowed my head in gratitude at the recognition. Jesus lit another cigarette, pushed the drum away from him and took my hand again. This time he pressed it to his lips briefly. I laughed and bowed my head softly. I could feel the love emanating from him. The respect he offered was not missed for a moment. I felt the familiar bond that musicians share with each other. I knew that I had a new brother of rhythm sitting in front of me. I knew also that today would be my gateway to a new family in Cuba.

One of the men who had been standing at the gate entered the patio. He spoke with Ishmael for some time before joining Jesus and I at the drums. He was Spanish looking, lighter skinned, with sandy brown hair and a distinguished air about him. He looked like a scholar of some kind.

Much to my surprise, in perfect English he said to me, "Hello. My name is Jose Luiz. Ishmael is my friend and neighbor. He asked me to come here to talk with you. He says you want to learn about the Religion and the drum, and that your Spanish is not so good. Is there anything I can help you with?"

I was touched by the eloquence of his speech. I felt an overwhelming sense of gratitude to Ishmael for thinking of this way to help me on what was only my second day in Cuba. I thanked Jose Luiz and the two of us spent a few minutes getting acquainted. I let him know that I would love it if he could be there with me for some of the classes, at least until my Spanish improved a little bit. I expressed how important it was to me that I really understood the meanings of things, especially in regard to the Religion.

"Ishmael wants you to learn as much as you can from him. I will help you. Anytime you don't understand something, he can call for me. I am in the house just across the street. We want you to understand things. It's important that you understand. I heard you play, you are a musician, like us. You're safe and in very good

hands here. You have found a family here with us, and you chose well in Ishmael. You will see and learn many things if you listen and watch carefully."

Another man came back into the courtyard, aged and a bit weary looking, but joyful in his expression. He embraced all of us with ardor before sitting down across from me, to study me carefully with scrutiny. He had also heard Jesus and I play. He seemed deeply intrigued and somewhat amused by me, like he would be with a young child. I instantly loved this man. He was wise, soft tender and while he was older, like a grandfather, he had an incredibly youthful spirit. His name was also Jesus. It was a few days later before I learned that he was the younger Jesus's father. It was even longer before I learned that these two men were renowned as master musicians in that part of Cuba and Jesus, Sr. was Jesus Morales Lima, well known as a famous composer of Afro-Cuban Orisha Music.

The five of us sat in Ishmael's courtyard together for several hours that first day together getting acquainted, laughing, playing and singing together until almost sunset. It was in this first day of learning and sharing with *Jesusito*, (the Jr. Jesus) that he told me that people come to Santeria for healing. He said that he was absolutely certain that I was called to Cuba to heal something inside of myself. He could not have been more right on. That something that needed healing was my broken heart.

When Frank came for me to walk home, he found me on the porch with Ishmael, rocking in the government issued rocker feeling more at home than I had anywhere in many years.

Jose was right, I had found a new family here through the love of music and song, and on day two in Cuba, I knew my life would never again be the same.

Spirit Speaks

The night is cold and no light comes from the sky. My hands hit the skin of my djembe with precision. A clear knowingness that comes from another time and place flows through me. The intensity of the drumming is fed by the fire blazing into the black of night, and the dancers pounding their feet into the earth all around us. Voices and songs from other worlds sing through me, as I surrender willingly to the remembrances that always find me here in the temple of rhythm, fire and ceremony.

I am flanked and backed on all sides by strong warrior-like men relentlessly marking time on their drums. Men who I have known and trusted in our work as drummers for countless ceremonies over the past decade. Together, over the years, we have shed blood, sweat and tears around these fires. Together we have played up the sun for days and weeks upon end. Tonight, however, is uncharted territory.

There is an unspoken seriousness in the ethers, as if we are at war with some unknown invisible dark force. We are playing in the fields of the keepers of the other worlds, fighting to bring light into the darkness.

A dancer emerges from out of the hundreds of bodies circling the fire in time to the rhythms we keep. She is swirling wildly towards me, calling on me to ride the rhythm with her tonight. My hands instinctively respond, inspiring her movements just as

she inspires mine. She is dressed in pure white, as am I, and my brothers on either side of me.

She pulls the white veil over her head and enters the portal of rhythm we begin to create together. Her movements and the rhythms from my drum become one expression, taking her higher and higher into her trance. From the distance a piercing scream shatters the night. The fire goes cold, almost disappearing into the darkness.

Suddenly my world goes dark. My head drops. I feel powerless. My body goes limp. I am still playing, doggedly holding onto the rhythm for the dancer, but a heaviness has come over me. I hear my brother call to me, but he sounds worlds away. I can still feel the connection with the dancer, and the drummers around me, yet I am suddenly transported to another place, a hundred yards behind myself, at the opening to a large tent.

My hands hold metal: in one hand a stick, and in the other a bell. I am standing perfectly still witnessing a man, hunched over in a chair being lashed with a horsetail on his head, shoulders and back. He looks weakened, as if his spirit is being taken over by darkness and confusion. It feels as if I am hovering; the stick in my right hand clanging heavily against the bell in my left hand playing a 6/8 pattern known as short bell with a pronounced fierceness, and yet no one looks up at me. There are several other people milling around in the tent. A large man towers above them all, his arms waving wildly as he thrashes the other man with the horsetail. His drama is entrancing them. His eyes are bulging out. He is intimidating and overpowering. I realize suddenly, in that moment, that the source of the darkness we are up against tonight comes from this tent.

I am fearless. I step closer and play louder, hoping to distract him, to let him know he has been seen. I know no darkness can stand in the face of pure light. Still no one seems to notice me. I stand ten feet from the opening watching, playing loudly, and then singing. A song comes through me in a language I do not

know, from some other place and time that my soul remembers well.

I know this large man. I know he claims to be a practitioner and priest of Santeria. Everything in my blood boils as I stand watching this debacle unfold. I know very little of Santeria, yet somehow this feels like an insult to a proud and beautiful religion and tradition. Somehow, it feels like sickness: a manipulation, a commercialized dramatization of something that at its core is integral and pure. A voice from the Spirit world speaks to me, not in words, but in thought. The message is crystal clear. It receives no resistance from me as I witness this sick display of Americans playing with an ancient religion and confusing it for some theatre of power over others. The message to me is strong: "Anything you learn of The Religion, you must learn only from the Pure, and only from a place of its Roots: only in Cuba or Africa."

Another primal scream shatters the night. This one is deep and thunderous, as it echoes through the night. I feel my own mouth closing. It was my voice piercing the shadow of night. My voice calling forth the light. As I open my eyes, I see the fire shoot up into the sky. My body straightens at the drum. I notice a hand on the small of my back, supporting and holding me up from behind. My brothers next to me scream out "GO! GO! GO!" The dancer, still in front of me, leaps into the air in response to the blast of rhythm and song that continues to flow out of me. After the energy is stabilized strong, I release my drum. I jump into the dance around the fire, taking the dancer's hand in mine. Hundreds of voices respond with ecstasy as the first light of dawn emerges. The energy builds to a frenzied cacophony of rhythm, song and movement.

The light has returned. Dawn arrives.

Ceremony

"Be careful when you go there. You might see things you've never seen before, things that might frighten you. I've been watching the way you are. Your heart is very open. You must take care when you go there. You must protect yourself. Not everyone is your friend here. You must always remember that."

I nodded and watched as Frank tensed up in the background, while Jose Luiz spoke to me in perfect English, just minutes before we were to leave for my first official Santeria ceremony to go to another village close to Cojimar.

It was my fourth day on the island of Cuba. My mind was less concerned with protecting myself, than it was on wondering where in the world Jose learned to speak such perfect English living here in Cojimar, Cuba. Cojimar is a quaint village on the outskirts of Havana. It seems no one speaks even a word of English here. No one, that is, except Jose. Jose had instantly become part of my support team here to help me when my brain became overwhelmed trying to speak and understand the lightning fast Cuban Spanish.

I was still listening intently to Jose's well intended speech, curious on what I might be going to witness. From the way he was depicting it, I envisioned a huge crowd of people somewhere out in the middle of the forest, all dressed in white, dancing and drumming furiously in the hot sun, with the blood curdling screams of sacrificial animals ringing through the air.

I really had no idea what I was getting myself into. I also knew that I most definitely was not afraid. I was only excited and filled with tremendous anticipation and a sense of adventure.

"Thank you, Jose." I said with my hand on my heart and a smile in my eyes. "I will be careful. My heart is always open, but I will also keep my eyes open. I promise." He smiled and touched me gently on the shoulder as he walked past me to the gate.

I knew he was just looking out for me and I sincerely appreciated his concern. The truth was that I was clueless as to where I was going, and what I was heading into. I was putting

all my trust in Ishmael to take good care of Frank and I. I knew Frank was scared shitless, by his own admission, but more so by the wide-eyed frozen bunny stare he found my eyes through time and time again as we loaded up in the street in front of Ishmael's house. He was willing to accompany me despite his fears. I appreciated that as well. His presence was comforting in spite of his fears.

I had only been in Cuba a few days. I think he thought I was a little crazy for saying yes to the invitation to attend a Santeria Ceremony, especially with someone I had just met and barely knew.

The fact that I was invited at all was a sweet surprise to me. Yet, here I was, day four on the island heading into a world of mystery, magic and music. I felt honored that these doors were opening to me so quickly. Ishmael had been carefully watching me during my classes, and I trusted his intuitive guidance.

The world of Santeria is a protected world. One that many are never granted access to even after years of visiting the island. I have many friends who have visited Cuba over the years who were never invited to an authentic ceremony. Many of them were coerced into paying hundreds of dollars before being allowed to see what was really just a commercial version of a ceremony, made for the eyes of tourists only.

I am fully aware that it is a great honor to be invited in as an outsider, especially after only a few days here. What is even more beautiful is that there have been no requests or talk of money. I know that I am being invited as a guest and in the purest of ways: as a sister of the rhythm and a lover of spirit.

Ishmael, Frank, Jesus, Jesucito, and I pile into the faded blue 1953 Chevy taxi. I offer a quick silent prayer that we all return safe and sound. I am not afraid, yet after Jose's warning, I notice I do feel a slight bit of anxiety laced with a growing curiosity, that stimulates all kinds of imaginative thoughts.

I realize for a moment how vulnerable I truly am. I had just met these men. Frank speaks less Spanish than I do, which is to

say none. No one in the car speaks a word of English. I have no idea where we are going, what to expect, if I am dressed properly, what will happen, when we are coming back, when and what I will eat, and I am absolutely loving the adventure of it all. I feel alive, powerful, present and completely safe from any danger.

I love passing through the villages of Cuba. The colors are so stark, brilliant and playful. The surreal combination of decay and vibrancy is a striking visual experience, an eye candy I never knew I was missing. I love seeing the old men and women standing on their front stoops smoking cigars, with tired deep lines in their faces and hopelessness spread across their furrowed brows. I love how fast that hopelessness transforms to joy when a neighbor calls out to them. The joy in life here comes primarily through friends, community and connection with each other. People literally live to share and connect. There is little else to give their lives purpose outside of the connections with each other. This strikes a chord of resonance in me as one of the forgotten truths of humanity.

A horse and carriage packed with vegetables passes us. I want to reach out, and grab something to eat. I giggle inside at the thought of a vegetarian in Cuba, recalling the responses I get here when I say, "No como carne." Cubans look at me with this blank look on their face, as if I just said I am an alien. "Bah, no entiendo. Porque?" (I don't understand. Why?) is the usual response.

We eventually pull up in front of a house. After all the vivid imaginations that have been running through my mind, I am assuming we are stopping to pick someone else up.

We're certainly not in the forest. We are right in the middle of an average looking Cuban neighborhood.

Everyone piles out of the car. I offer money for the taxi. Ishmael looks at me as if I've just kicked him. He says firmly, "No," and pushes my money back towards me. We cross the street and enter a bright pink concrete house. "What are we doing here?" Frank says.

"I don't know. I guess we're about to find out." I say. I am almost annoyed now that Frank is with me. He is so visibly uncomfortable, and so stiff, it is almost embarrassing. At the same time, I am also really happy he's here to have someone to speak English with and to laugh with me a little along the way. His presence is still comforting despite the annoyances of his anxieties. I choose to rest in gratitude.

I realize this is where the ceremony is happening when I peek in and see altars, candles and flowers placed around the periphery of the room and a bowl of rose water by the door. The drums start almost immediately. The people in the room re-arrange themselves, stop talking and start to move in time to the rhythms. I bend down and take a little of the sacred water, tap it on my forehead and behind my head, and invite Frank to do the same.

"I think I'm going to go sit over there and write." He says. He leaves and sits across the street outside on the pavement in the hot sun. I shrug my shoulders and enter the house. I am the only pale skinned one there. No one seems to even notice me, and no one goes out of their way to greet me. I am tolerated, but clearly and politely ignored. I notice the warmth in my heart and remind myself of Jose's words. I commit to keeping my eyes open even though I want to close them, sink in and pray with them.

The first song has started already. My teachers, Jesus and Jesucito, are leading the songs and chorus, flanked by three other drummers.

I find myself giggling inside about Jose's warning and all the imaginations that my mind created from it. I do not doubt for a moment that such things happen as he was warning me of, but this is clearly not what today's ceremony will be about.

My body starts to feel the rhythms I intrinsically love so much, moving me from the inside out. I instinctively start to sway and step in time. There are maybe 40 people there, all packed into the small living room. An elder woman sits in the corner, near the altar, with burning candles, bottles of rum and sweets.

The ceremony is clearly for her. She looks weak and exhausted, slumping in her chair. I presume she is sick.

The songs come one after another. The space in front of the drummers is packed with dancing bodies, all moving in time to the music, and echoing the calls of the "cantos" (songs) that Jesus is belting out over the drums. The intensity continues to build. This is home to me. I feel the familiar dropping in of Spirit. I suddenly remember the night, years ago around a fire in Florida, where I was first guided to find my way to Cuba to experience Santeria firsthand.

I cringe inside at how Americans seem to bastardize and corrupt the purity of other culture's religions for profit and personal power. I pray that this world, here in Cuba, remains protected and pure for generations to come. As the ceremony opens, I am offering my own prayers, clapping, singing, dancing and feeling profound gratitude. I feel comfortable, safe, powerful and at home here. I feel seen and intimately connected, even though no one knows my name.

It is hot in the little room and everyone is dripping with sweat. The woman in the corner starts to sway. When the rhythm and singing gets wild and furious, she finally pops to her feet and starts swaggering about. Everyone makes space for her, clapping and singing as she enters the trance fully. She falls back into me. I support her with my hands, gently popping her back into the center to continue her work.

I know this world. I know exactly how to be here. I have never been in a ceremony like this before, yet somehow, I know it. It is beyond familiar. It feels like something I have done a million times. I feel more comfortable and safe here, than I have anywhere in years.

I notice now that the people are looking at me differently when they meet my eyes. I am sweating and dancing with them, following their footwork. We are praying together. There is no separation here. Here we all understand the same language. We do not need to say a word. The women are standing next to me,

dancing with me, giving me appreciative glances. Many people are now smiling at me when I look up. I know they may be curious about me, but more than that; I know that I am received fully now as part of a family of spirit beyond my skin color or cultural past. It all happens in the music and movement in a moment.

A few people are led out of the room when their trance gets too heavy or when they collapse on the floor. Some land in the arms of someone in the room and are supported until they regain their balance, and can continue dancing or stand on their own again. Two women faint completely. They are taken out of the room. The elder woman is smiling now. She seems transformed completely. She looks light on her feet, rejuvenated and alive. The healing power of rhythm and song has done its job.

After a few hours, the drumming stops and everyone files outside to get fresh air. It ends as unceremoniously as it began. Plastic cups filled with hot soup are passed around. Even though I am a vegetarian, I drink it down, knowing it is chicken or pork and that it was likely sacrificed on site.

Frank is sitting across the street, smiling and playing with two little children. As I wipe the sweat off my brow, I feel reborn. Iam home again. I feel complete and happy.

Ishmael comes out with a huge smile on his face and embraces me heartily, laughing and pulling me close to him. I feel like we've known each other for years. It's only been a few days. Real connections are like that for me, just undeniably effortless. The women come out and hug and kiss me. They start chatting with me as if we have known each other forever. The men pat me on the back, or kiss me on the cheek, as if I am their sister. The feeling of kinship is very real and present amongst us all.

Jesus Sr. wobbles out, his 73-year-old body moving slowly towards me. With a huge smile on his face, kisses me on the cheek ardently. His son Jesucito, follows right behind with a cigarette in his thin fingers, and a cup of rum in his hand. He hands me the rum and hugs me, "Ah Cheri! Dale!" I drink the

rum joyfully knowing it is an honor to be offered the cup of the Master Drummer to drink from.

I am so filled with love. I am complete.

The ceremony is finished. We are all purified and whole again. We pile in the car and with incessant chatter, laughter and smiles. We take the journey back to Cojimar as family reconnected through Rhythm's embrace.

Glimpses In Havana Real

Havana Real is a secret world,
hidden from the view of tourists and passersby's.

Inside of it are thousands of people, souls, animals and secrets
crawling around in the skeletons of these old buildings.

It is a living, breathing museum to explore where the ghosts of
Cuba's thick past linger in stairways, alleys and balconies,
keeping watch over their still majestic city.

The streets of Havana are tight and congested, and so brilliantly perfect, despite the stench of decay and trash that fills the air. It is a living, breathing museum to explore where the ghosts of Cuba's thick past linger in stairways, alleys and balconies, keeping watch over their still majestic city.

I can almost see the women with their bustiers, and the men with their top hats, spilling onto the cobblestone streets of Havana. Here black faced musicians are singing and dancing in the crowded taverns and paladors. I look up to the balconies and see the ghosts of the eras hanging over the sides, watching the city's action, smoking cigars and sucking down bottles of rum.

Havana is an inexplicably alluring city. Its history is such a wildly bustling blend of stories, characters, magic, mystery, traumas and dramas. Once a wealthy city filled with gambling, whorehouses, traders, mobsters, sailors, imperialists, and wealthy Spaniards, French and then Americans; the Havana of today is a treasure chest filled with the unexpected to explore.

The mix of Cuba's glory days with its multiple revolutions, create a dynamic tapestry from which modern Cuba is working still to break free from. Havana truly is the heart of Cuba and has been the primary stage for the stories to unfold since the beginning of colonization in Cuba.

The architecture here sings songs of Cuba's past. The crumbling facades hold the choirs of the many cultures that have influenced Cuba's history. One can find amongst the glorious rubble hints of history from parts far and wide: Moorish, Spanish, Italian, Greek and Roman architecture are prevalent. From the colonial and baroque periods to the more modern era, with the drab tower blocks of Russian origin, balancing out the beauty with their dullness. The history of Havana is boldly represented in every way in its unique concrete jungle.

Once proud majestic buildings, these gorgeous structures now exist in various states of decay and degradation. Many of these buildings are literally crumbling. Occasionally one

collapses entirely with a thunderous rumble. Eyes widen and within moments, wailing cries can be heard as neighbors run to the rescue of the inhabitants who may have been trapped inside. Often, even worse, they arrive to find their beloveds crushed beneath the rubble.

What most tourists will never know about Havana is that there are secret and vast worlds living behind the crumbling walls of decay. Hordes of tourists pass by taking photos of these old buildings not knowing they are just the fa<ade of Havana Real. Just behind those walls, worlds upon worlds cascade into hidden courtyards and communities where the real life of Havana's people happens.

The inner world of what I call "Havana Real", is a maze of tiny compartmentalized micro-apartments, literal holes in the wall that reek of urine, feces and cigar smoke. Within Havana Real, lives a deep, unseen poverty of its own kind, with its own ghosts, stories and profound expressions of humanity. Havana Real is a secret world, hidden from the view of tourists and passerby's, and inside of it, are thousands of people, souls, animals and secrets crawling around in the skeletons of those old buildings.

In Havana Real many Cubans and their families live in often unsafe and sometimes deadly worlds. Old pipes and peeling paint and rickety rotting stairwells barely held in place by makeshi" scaffolding are the norm. Lead poisoning, and poor or no plumbing leading to health and sanitation challenges are just an accepted parts of daily life for those who have carved out a home in this surreal maze. Here, behind the majestic facades the tourists see in streets, it is not uncommon to hear the stories of those who have died in this world when the walls come crumbling in on them.

My new friend Mariella lives amongst this maze. I met Mariella at a restaurant that I stopped at one day for a snack in Havana. She was the server there and took my order. She was very interested in hearing about my trip to Cuba. When she learned of my interest in The Religion, she immediately invited me to

visit her family. She was a little quiet and looked around often when we spoke at the restaurant, but her hesitancy and shyness completely dissolved as we walked away from her workplace towards her home several blocks away.

I fell in love with her instantly. Mariella is a tiny woman with the tiniest of tiny feet. She speaks extra slow to me so that I can understand every word. I enjoy being able to understand the words one by one. It gives me a false sense of confidence that maybe I'm starting to learn the language. The only problem is that she speaks so slowly, that by the time she gets to the end of the sentence, I have been so absorbed in the word to word comprehension that I have completely forgotten the previous words she spoke. The result being that I am almost as lost as I would have been if she were to speak at warp speed.

It is Mariella who introduced me to the world behind the walls that I nicknamed "Havana Real." The first day she brought me to her home, we walked from the restaurant for about 25 minutes, before she stopped abruptly and said to me, "Aqui es mi casa." We were standing next to what appeared to me to be a solid wall. There was no door, no entrance, nothing that looked at all like a home or apartment to me. I must have looked as baffled as I felt.

She stepped in front of me, with her tiny feet, took my hand in hers, and slipped into a crack in the wall. I was drawn into a world I could never have imagined existed. We slid through the crack for about ten feet before the sky opened a little. I saw that we were in a complex, a kind of inner courtyard. There were people and critters crawling around everywhere. Above me was scaffolding that looked like it could fall on us if we exhaled at all.

After sliding through the crack in the outer façade of her building from the street, I had to literally slither into her apartment. Getting through the doorway required me to bend and maneuver around the inward opening door, and enter carefully, one leg at a time. If I had been carrying even a small bag, I would have had to pass the bag in ahead of myself. The

opening was that small. A person of any substantial size would not fit thru her doorway, much less get into the building where the crack meets the street. The doorway was about three feet high, and more like a cubbyhole entrance than a true doorway.

Once inside, Mariella introduced me to her husband and three children who all lived inside of this very small, makeshift, cubbyhole apartment. No one could stand up straight except the children. I wondered how they got the small couch and table in through that opening. There was very little else inside. A small fridge, a burner and a silver espresso coffee pot, and of course, a TV and an altar.

Her children stared at me with curiosity and sat next to me. They were so excited to have a guest, and a foreigner at that. They played with my hair and had a sweet way of softly touching my hand or my leg when they spoke. I was humbled by the tenderness between Mariella and her husband. I could feel the love between them as they spoke. They too softly touched each other from time to time.

They had a gentle way with each other and with their children that spoke of enduring profound hardships together with a disciplined spiritual awareness, grace and dignity.

We sat together and talked for hours in that little cubbyhole apartment in Havana Real, laughing, learning about each other together and just being. They shared videos on The Religion with me, going into great detail to explain everything to me as slowly as possible, and in as much detail as possible. They would pause the video and stop and share with me, and invite me to ask questions. They made me coffee and offered me food, and let me know that they were my friends, and if I needed anything while I was in Havana, to please ask them.

Mariella and her husband clearly love their culture and their roots. They hold a deep passion for The Religion, and also considered themselves Catholic. They are well educated and highly intelligent people who could talk with me about almost any topic with insight and profound awareness of deeper issues,

politics, philosophy and humanity. I found this to be very common in Cuba.

The Cuban people are proud of their roots, and their history as a country of multiple revolutions. They are eager and happy to share what they know with outsiders. Furthermore, they have a genuine interest in hearing other perspectives, and learning from others through inquiry and conversation. The Cuban people value the direct sharing and experience of humanity more than book knowledge and media propaganda. They want to understand more of the world outside of Cuba through the voices and eyes of those of us who live on the outside.

They are also masters at reading someone's character and spirit. I notice, time and time again, that the people here see me in a way that people of my own culture do not. They see my heart almost instantly. I often feel like they understand me in ways that I do not even fully understand myself in moments. It is as if, perhaps because of their history and struggles, they have a looking glass that peers into the deeper parts of humanity more organically than we tend to in the USA.

Our cultural dogma and societal structure require us to stay focused on income and production to survive. It lures us into the game of increasing material gain at the cost of time with those we love. We are constantly trying to maintain some certain standard that is supposed to signify success. As a whole, our culture is more concerned with this striving for success than we are the real-life experiences of humanity in the most pure and simple of forms. Our system has created the option and opportunity for extreme individualism, and individual independence.

Humanity as a deeper experience of sharing life's deeper meaning, and caring for each other and the planet has been traded in as a commodity. The price is our life and mental well-being. Our humanity has been slowly chipped away at, cheapened, and devalued greatly. It has now become a necessity for Americans to neurotically continue to strive for more and more for a lower

quality of life. The cost of living, at even a very basic standard, continues to skyrocket.

This incessant striving is proving only to disconnect us more from humanity and each other. Depression, mental illness, and deeper psychological disturbances are growing at an alarming rate in the modern world.

Mariella's family, and many other Cubans I met grasp this distinction fully. Extreme independence and individual survival tactics are uncommon and impractical on this island. There is an interdependence that is not only needed here for survival, but that is deeply cherished and enjoyed by most Cuban people as an expression of their shared humanity. Neighbors and families go through intense trials and challenges together. They find creative solutions to learn to co-exist in harmony. It's not la-la land by any means, yet because of their forced struggles and lack of resources, Cubans have mastered certain aspects of humanity that we are now becoming deeply deficient in in modern culture.

Stepping into Havana Real from time to time during my stay was always a joy, allowing me access to a simple sharing of humanity. I know many people would enter this world and only see poverty and hardship. Many would cringe and find it a world of horrors, and feel sorry for the people there. The truth is, even seeing the material deficiencies and how hard it was for them in some ways to live like this, there was never a moment when I thought of them as poor.

Mariella's family and all those I met in her world, had dignity, grace, and so much love to share that what I really experienced there was a richness that transcends the material plane. It is a wealth that creates kings and queens of another domain entirely.

Havana Heat

Groups of sculpted young men hover on the streets.

They devour me with their eyes as I walk past,
penetrating me to my core with their wanton lust.

I cannot deny that I have begun to enjoy it.

Havana Heat is a slow smoldering fire
burning away the past forever.

I am going to visit Mariella again today. I know she has been missing me. My only real problem, so far, in Cuba, is that I have too many friends and it is hard to keep up with them all. I adore them all. Once they realize I can speak even a little Spanish, they are bubbling over with enthusiasm to share with me. They have a burning desire to get to know more about my life and the outside world.

Popping off the bus, I walk through the square of the Capitol and head off on a journey through the streets of this magical city with a smile in my heart and a ripening curiosity for what lays ahead today. Mariella lives deep in Central Havana. There are so many people on the streets here that I have become quite comfortable walking alone.

Hordes of half naked man flesh greet my appreciative eye as I move through what many would call the ghettos or barrios of Cuba. Women walking with bags of groceries, and children playing in the streets with sticks and balls meet my smile with theirs.

Groups of sculpted young men hover on the streets playing dominos, fixing their bici-taxis or old cars, or just shooting the shit with friends. They devour me with their eyes as I walk past, penetrating me to my core with their wanton lust. I cannot deny that I have begun to enjoy it. Their playful sexual energy keeps a primal lust alive in me in spite of my broken heart. It feels good, and even healthy to just enjoy it all from a safe distance.

The now familiar kissing sounds they all make in my direction do not even faze me anymore. I quite often now return them in playful acknowledgement of the Cuban Culture. These besitos are a greeting I am beginning to love. When I was coming from my own biased, cultural assumptions, I took it as harassment and had a little chip on my shoulder about it. My liberation from the thought that it was just another degrading male to female expression came when I opened my eyes to see that this kissing sound is a playful way of saying, "Hey, I see you. You're beautiful.

I appreciate you." It's not just men doing it to women, its women to women, men to men, brother to sister, mother to son. What I discovered is that while it can be a form of flirting, it is more of a light-hearted acknowledgement: a casual playful expression of love, family and appreciation.

I have become more fearless than ever in Cuba. I know that as long as I maintain a certain energetic boundary here that I will always be safe. I know that not one of these sexy lust-driven men would dare to touch or harm me in any way, and that if one did, there would be hordes of others there to protect and defend me.

Being fair, if I were a Cuban woman, I might feel a little differently. There are several reasons I can feel safe enough to walk alone at any time as an outsider. For one, there are always so many people around, it's hard to get away with too much mischief here. The Cubans talk openly about the cameras that are on many of the buildings and streets to monitor security and keep an eye on people. Tourists are heavily protected by Cuban law. Attacking a tourist holds a very heavy penalty which can include imprisonment, and can even be punishable by death under certain circumstances. Havana and Cuba are so safe now because the government here does not play.

On the more socio-psychological level, no one really wants to be ostracized from their community or family, or singled out as a bad guy here. Trust, integrity and taking care of each other are integral requirements to maintain the community connections. This ties back into that interdependence I mentioned earlier.

Everyone here needs each other and so there is an innate respect and order to the culture that works from the inside out.

This makes Cuba a glorious place for a single woman to travel and enjoy a freedom that she may have never experienced anywhere in her entire life. There are very few places in the world where a woman can walk the streets at night and be safe, and even fewer where rape has such serious penalties as in Cuba.

The liberation in it is an incredible experience. Even still, I keep a comfortable, safe distance from these steamy hot, sculpted

bodies that call out to me along my walk. It's so deeply ingrained in me to be protective. As a woman, I must always keep my guard up, even here in Cuba.

The men here are supremely sexy. I cannot help but appreciate them. Cubans come in every color from white to deep black. I love them all, although I think the café colored chocolate is my favorite. Their skin is smooth, sleek and shiny, it looks almost edible. The sexual magnetism they ooze, combined with their confidence and stature is undeniably powerfully intriguing.

It was in Havana on a casual stroll with Ishmael that I first got a physical understanding and visceral experience of what the phrase, "weak in the knees" truly means. Being such a strong empowered women, I scoffed at that concept. I had always considered it just a colloquial silliness in statement. On a hot day in Havana, I got a true blue chemistry lesson that left me literally staggering to stand up.

He wore long dreads tied up on his head. He wasn't a particularly standout kind of guy to be honest. His skin was my favorite cafe color. Round John Lennon specs framed the most exquisite face and soul piercing eyes I had ever seen. He breezed past us, and met my eyes for only a few moments before passing by me. That was it. No other interaction whatsoever. He passed about three feet from me. When he did I literally went weak in the knees and had to grab onto Ishmael to not fall to the ground.

It was such a powerful chemical reaction that it nearly knocked me over. Ishmael looked at me with his eyebrow raised, and we both laughed as I grabbed his arm. "Cubano por ti? Dale!" he said encouraging me to follow the man.

"No hermano, Los Cubanos son demaciado peligrosos por me amor. Aye Calor." I responded through my laughter. He mockingly fanned me for a few moments, smiling. He held me up and still giggling, we turned and kept walking arm in arm towards the taxis.

I meet up with Mariella a few hours later, and we take a walk to a café in Havana Vieja for coffee. I know she does not get to

enjoy this kind of luxury often. I am happy to take her out for some relaxation on her day off. It is my favorite restaurant in Havana. The ceiling is covered with live plants and vines that spread across the open-air trellised roof. The European influence of the building, architecture and décor is strong here. The place feels classy but not overdone; elegant and delightfully Cuban.

I can see Mariella is out of her element and a little nervous. I assure her it is not that expensive and that it is OK for her to order whatever she likes. She sits down with a huge smile on her face like a child having a first experience. I am touched and so happy to share this moment with my new friend.

Halfway through our meal, I notice my heart racing a little and wonder if it is just the coffee making me feel flushed. I feel eyes on me. I look around and I do not see anyone watching me, but my sixth sense is activated. I have learned to always be mindful of this feeling as a woman traveling alone. This does not feel like danger, but it still gets my attention. Someone is most definitely watching me.

After some time chatting, Mariella and I leave. I let the feeling subside as the wind picks up and much to my delight, Oya tosses banyan leaves in front of us, and over our heads. It's a moment of Disney-like magic with the leaves swirling around her tiny little feet and falling down around us. The night air is cool and the wind is comforting. The sense of sisterhood between she and I is strong and sweet. I feel gratitude for the moments we have shared. We walk arm in arm, laughing as we wander through the streets of Havana like old friends.

A few blocks down the road, she meets one of her neighbors, and since night has fallen, she insists I go directly to get a taxi rather than walking her back home. She does not want me having to walk back out of the barrio alone. I have walked probably more than five miles today, so I do not argue. A leisurely stroll alone to the Malecon, (the seaside) sounds quite romantic. We embrace and exchange a kiss on the cheek, and go our separate ways both touched by our day together.

The night is heaven here. It is perfect. I have been enjoying the romance I have been having with myself on this trip. I feel romantic enough to treat myself to a glass of red wine before I return to my safe haven in Cojimar. Returning to the same cafe, I take a table by the street on the patio. As soon as I sit down, that sixth sense kicks in again and the hair on the back of my neck rises a little bit.

Right now, I do not care that someone is watching me. I feel 20 feet tall and cherished by myself. I pat myself on the back internally for all the work and processing I have been doing to feel again like the Queen of my own domain. I order a glass of red wine and let the love and wine wash through me. My eyes soften. My body sinks into the moment. A warmth moves through me. I am once again feeling pleasured by the soft sweet kisses of Oya's cool night embrace. My beloved lover, she is always here for me.

The warmth slowly turns into an intense burning heat with a surreal psychic embrace that kind of pops me back to my senses. I am most definitely being watched. My first impulse is to get my bill and dash off, but a wave of defiance rolls over me. I relax inside, remembering that I am safe here.

"Ah, let them watch," my bitch queen thinks. Who could blame a man for appreciating a woman who is in love with life and herself? An inspired woman in her prime getting off on the wind isn't something most of them see every day anyway. I smile laughing inside at my silly, sassy self chatter. I sit up in my chair anyway, shifting to a slightly protective space.

The truth is, no man stands a chance with me right now. My ex ripped a hole in my heart big enough to swallow the whole of the universe. Now that it is starting to heal, I am quite content alone. I will therefore let him watch and appreciate a woman in love with herself.

The heat of Havana's eyes warms me to my core tonight.

I wander back into the night feeling sensually alive as the breath of cuba tosses the leaves across my feet again.

Oya's Breath

I am relieved to receive her when I feel her stirring on my skin.
It has been a very quiet morning and I found myself longing
for her. Awakening early without her breath had me feeling the
emptiness of a melancholy despair.

I found myself lying in bed for a long time awaiting her return,
dreaming of visiting her in her world.

Flying between the worlds, I am with her: whisking over the
ocean, creating white frenzied waves out of calm glassy seas,
pushing myself through the spaces between
the leaves of every tree and slipping sensually through the palm
fronds, delightfully aroused by their soft touch, as they sway
and dance hypnotically at her command.

Oya. She is the ultimate lover. I awaken with a smile inside.

Another beautiful day of magic is unfolding. Enjoying my morning café and reflecting on my trip, I find myself smiling inside reliving a moment. I had gone to the fruit stand to pick up some bananas for my day, and the man who worked there said to me, "Cubana si?"

"No," and I laughed. "Americana amigo." I couldn't believe he actually thought I was Cuban. How could that be? His response in perfect English surprised me even more, as very few people here in Cojimar speak English.

"Are you sure you're from the U.S.? You don't look or act like an American. You look like you live here. You act like one of us. So, you married a Cubano, si, and you live here then?"

"No friend. I came to visit for my first time. I have been here only for three weeks. I leave in three days. I am very sad to have to go." I responded to him.

It is true. I am incredibly sad to be leaving this rock in three days. I know my heart will stay here when my body goes and I will have to come back for it, to feed it over and over, until maybe one day I can stay.

The truth is that I feel more Cubana inside than Americana lately. I feel like this place just makes more sense to me on the humanistic level. Politics, economics and social systems all have their own messiness to them that I'll never fully grasp. They have never been the most important aspects of experiencing life's magic to me. There is plenty here that doesn't work or make sense in those realms, just as there is plenty in my own country that doesn't work or make sense to me. Politics and economics have always been surreal mysteries to me. I tend to see beyond them and not waste my life trying to understand the impossible.

In Cuba, however, the culture, and the way people interact on a day to day basis within the community context, seems much more normal, organic, and healthy on a lot of levels to me, than the way most people live in the good old USA. I understand the comfortable casual way that people relate and communicate

here. The pace of life feels more in alignment with my spirit. The warm, sultry nights and the easy way people have with each other makes sense to me. The music, dancing and the drumming are medicine to my body, mind and soul. The lack of technology and the natural lifestyle this culture embraces are a refreshing reminder of humanity's simplicity.

I have not missed cell phones or computers in the least. Remembering what it feels like to put pen to paper and write old-fashioned style, has actually been nourishing. I have found my writing time to be something I really look forward to. I enjoy sitting in one of the infamous government issued rocking chairs, watching the palm trees dance as the words fall onto the page from my hand. Returning to the United States feels like a huge inevitable disappointment I must face. I am already grieving.

To return to that world feels like treason to my soul. I keep praying that maybe somehow, I will get stuck here and have to stay. I find myself fantasizing that I will just disappear on this rock. I ponder how long it would take for me to fade into a memory in the lives of those I would leave behind. I wonder if I already have.

I close my eyes again. I let my self dream of a life where I can stay here and make love to the wind forevermore.

Rising In Love

I hear horse hooves snapping on the cobblestone streets. The
wind is carrying rhythms in her bosom once again. I can hear
the ocean lapping against the rocky shore.

My lover reaches his foot over to mine across the bed.
He pulls me close. In a moment his arms are wrapped
around me, holding me sweetly in the late afternoon glow
of our loving. Still I can not see his face.

"Amor," he whispers, "Amor siempre."
He tickles the back of my neck with his scruffy face.

I am smiling inside, feeling so warm, content and rested.

I drift back into a deep place within.

A voice breaks the silence as he rolls over to kiss my lips ever so lightly. I awake in bliss and curiosity once again. Who is this man? Why is that his face always eludes me in these dreams that haunt my early mornings? I wonder if he will always remain only in the dream worlds for me.

"Bah, men. Who needs 'em anyway," I hear my sarcastic wounded bitch say. I get up, amused at myself and laughing inside. I know I am moving into a place of healing, slowly, but with great wisdom. Not getting myself all wrapped up in another man is the best medicine for me and I know it.

Luckily, my sense of humor is still with me.

My thoughts return to where my body rests, in Cojimar, Cuba. I remember that Ishmael is making special tamales for me today. I quickly dress and suck down my morning coffee, before heading through the village to the house of my dear friend.

In the very near future, I will have to betray my spirit and return to the United States. My heart is aching with grief, and yet, I know with total certainty that I will return to this island as soon as I possibly can, and for much longer next time. Until then, I will live in the anticipation of the emergence of that moment. My teachers here say the village elders have been talking about initiating me into the Santeria Religion upon my return. I am not sure I am ready for that, but I am touched and honored that they have been discussing such things in my absence.

As I get ready to walk out the door, I am stopped by the image of a woman staring back at me with incredible love beaming from her face. I pause and take a moment to gaze and appreciate her. Her big green eyes stare right through me. Her eyes are filled with tenderness, strength and appreciation for this life. She looks joyful, at peace and capable of just about anything. I feel that she is blessing me by her gaze. "You really are a beautiful woman, my love," she says to me. I smile bowing to the Goddess that has returned to dwell in me at last.

She knows there were moments, in this past year, especially, when I could not bear to see the sight of myself. There were weeks and months filled with moments when I could not even glance in the mirror, much less look deeply into my own eyes as I am now. The reflection was just too sad and hurt to bear witness to. There were myriads of moments when looking too long only brought wild raging tears, a furious storm from within, and dizzying feelings of being precariously perched on the razor's edge between insanity and sanity.

I learned what it is like to live in my own version of hell, burning with self-hatred and vengeful thoughts of self-destruction and contempt. For better or worse, I have always been a bit of a warrior and even in my darkest moments, I have remained determined to not be afraid. I instead invited the demons of my mind to sit with me in purgatory. I asked them questions that gave me clues on how to understand them. I bid them to be of service to me somehow. I wondered if perhaps I were to befriend them, if they might indeed grant me safe passage without hurting anyone else along the way. This seemed like the most compassionate thing I could request from them and from myself. I discovered ultimately that it worked for me, and that nothing else really ever did.

I sat in patient knowingness, with them tearing at my eyes, making me blind to all but their sickness and delusions. I let them feast on my flesh until I became a skeleton of myself. I allowed them access to all my fears. They wasted no time in manifesting those same fears for me to witness, and somehow survive. Slowly, through my own continued willingness to accept the demons of my own mind, even to have compassion for their suffering and misery, even to love them for the lessons they offered and the wisdom that only true experience can offer, slowly they have been setting me free to live amongst the awakened angels again.

Occasionally, the darkness sings its melancholy melody through my soul to remind me of the demons that are, and always will be, willing to entertain me, if I so choose. They skirt

the edges of my bliss with glaring eyes and flesh ripping jowls, salivating for a taste of me.

It seems the closer my departure date from Cuba comes, the stronger their scent on the wind. They come as memories of the hurt, as visions of worst-case scenarios and fears of falling back into that pit of my past.

The knock on the door accompanied by Ishmael's sweet voice is just in time. I am ready to dance the demons back to their resting place once again. Using all the love I have for this beautiful queen whose reflection touches my heart now with adoration, I coerce them to bid me farewell, so that she may shine through me. Being loyal and kind to her means not heeding the calls to dance with the demons anymore.

Ishmael and I walk across the village arm in arm, all the way to his sister's home in Alamar for our feast of tamales. The steamy corn goodness melts in my mouth as Ishmael, his family, and I share in his creations. They are delicious, perfectly cooked and so delightful to enjoy. My heart feels tender and open. I find it hard to hold back tears as I watch my friend talking to his sister. The two of them are so graceful together, so comfortable and caring towards each other.

I cannot help but feel the hole in my heart. The pain around my lack of a relationship with my own brother is front and center even in my joy sharing with my friends.

I have always longed for the kind of comfort that Cubans find in their families. I have had to accept long ago that I may never have that kind of connection with my family. It may simply never be available to me with them. It's not because they are bad people in any way, but because there is no cultural context for the kind of family bonds that Cubans share. We don't have as much need for each other and there is very little, if any, interdependence amongst the members of my family.

I am not alone in this. Many American families are estranged, uncomfortable with each other and spend more time trying to avoid each other than seeking out the nurturance and enjoyment

of the simple sharing of life together. Often, one or more of the children in a family grow up, and move away, never to return. One day they will likely stick their aging parents in some kind of a nursing home. They will let someone else deal with them as they transition out of this life because they are too busy dealing with their own kids, who will likely do the same to them when they get older.

The system is not set up for us to take care of our own in the same way that Cubans do. In Cuba, it is a matter of survival. Everyone needs each other, and few people move too far from home. Family is the building block of community. Family is at the heart of the Cuban culture in so many ways.

I am, however, incredibly grateful for the brotherhood and sisterhood I have felt with so many others on the planet who are not blood family, but family of the heart. Through my love of music, community work, culture and the arts, I have experienced a profound sense of belonging. A sense of family and unity that is absolutely healing and nurturing. It is this family that has inspired my life on so many levels and given me a sense of deep kinship in this world.

I dry my tears and shake off the emotions to get back to the present moment. After all, tonight is a celebration for me. Ishmael worked all day to make tamales for me when he found out how much I love them. He even made them without meat, vegetarian style, just for me. I feel so blessed. My heart is bursting, it is so filled with love. A crystalline clarity moves through me knowing this is just the beginning of a lifelong love story.

Over and over on this journey, I have realized that the love affair I am having with Cuba is also an unfolding love affair with myself. I love the woman I am seeing myself as here. A brave woman that has shown up in this country where she knew no one. A woman who has let the powerful forces of love and loss become a therapeutic soup on a journey back to herself. I am experiencing myself now as a woman who was courageous enough to step into a dream and go for it, trusting in her own

abilities and in the Divine to support the journey, and keep her safe.

I love this woman who walks fearlessly through alleys and streets smiling, talking and sharing little moments of connection with the locals. This woman who, on a whim, responded to a possibility spontaneously presented, and hopped on a plane to explore an ancient cellular memory cracked open through drumming and midnight voices.

I love this woman. I know now, more now than ever, that she can do most anything if it is calling her. I love that she is a hopeless romantic who makes love with the wind and embraces the earth, who screams to the seas when she grieves, flashes fire through her eyes when she's angry, and who cries rivers of joy, love, and compassion freely. I am in love with her realness, her over-expressed, over-exposed heart, her raw and ripe willingness to splash the world with her passion. I am in awe of her strong, supple body, youthful, even as it ages, and always ready to dance when the music moves.

I see the depths of all of life and death in her eyes. The wisdom she carries shines through them. I feel blessed to walk this life with her. I am devoted to serving, and caring for her as my truest beloved. I will never again compromise her.

When I look up, I see Ishmael's hand extended and hear salsa music. He knows I do not dance salsa very well. I am a little intimidated, because he is such a masterful dancer. I know he is offering his hand to honor me and inviting me to dance just to play together. Although I am feeling totally inadequate and awkward, I get up smiling and meet him in the dance the best that I can. Ishmael's footwork is so smooth and so textured. I feel like a fumbling dork trying to keep up, but we laugh together and dance anyway.

I am slightly relieved when the music changes and his sister steps in to show me how it is done. It is so beautiful to watch them together. They move together perfectly. Years and years of dancing together like this have given them a comfortable

familiarity with each other that translates as blissful communion with life itself. Cubans grow up dancing together as family. There is no shame in sensuality or close intimate dancing for family members. It is a normal healthy sharing, even at very young ages.

We are all laughing together, as they move skillfully together in the tiny living room, showing off their mastery and enjoying every moment of it. I see their faces lighting up together, sharing in this love of music and movement that is such a powerful bond in their culture. In that moment, I make a commitment that when I return to Cuba, I will return knowing how to dance salsa.

A few hours later, Ishmael and I pack up and start on the long walk back to Cojimar from his sister's house in Alamar. I am full, radiantly happy and completely content. A soft gentle breeze comes across the water as we walk together laughing like children.

Ishmael stops and looks at me when the wind starts, "Cheri, dime: Oya? Ella habla contigo a menudo?" (Cheri, tell me, Oya, does she speak with you much?).

I laugh a little, feeling a little bit exposed, but also very safe with him. He knows the Orishas, and I remember that the first night we met he had noticed when the winds changed after we spoke. I know Ishmael is deeply tuned to the spirit world. It was evident immediately that he sees me in a way that few other people ever have in this life.

I pause for a moment, and look into his curious face before I respond with my hand on my heart. "Si Amor. Si. Ella es duena de me Corazon."

For a moment, the wind is still.

We share in a timeless moment, eye-to-eye, heart-to-heart with Oya as our only witness, silently acknowledging us in her bosom. We are two people from such different worlds. A big black man and a tiny white woman standing by the water in silence. Our hearts are connected by something that neither of us can put into words; something etheral, timeless and infinite that lives within each of us. As the moon shimmers across the

sea, we are swimming in this knowingness that goes beyond time and form. We are suspended in the space between Oya's breath, held by a connection that needs no definition, but that defines the truth of who we are.

He takes my hand in his and presses it to his heart with a gentle bow.

Oya sends us on our way with the softest of kisses through a sweet gentle breath. We walk the rest of the way home listening to her song.

Cuba's Dance of Romance

The magic of romance calls the dance forth.

Divinity finds home in sacred flirtatiousness: a courtship dance that demonstrates the attraction of the masculine to the feminine, her acknowledgment of his desire, and the sensual sweet play of a man and a woman exploring their attraction together.

She invites him through flirtatious looks, hip swirls,
shoulder shimmy's, booty shakes and smiles.

He uses all his skills of coercion, with dignity and respect, combined with as much charm and stamina as he has to try to win her affection.

Rhumba

I love the way men here show their respect and care for women. Chivalry is not dead here, not even close. I am always offered a hand when I get on a bus, or in and out of a car. Even if there is just a step up to take on the sidewalk, my companions will always reach back to be sure I can get my dainty foot over that four-inch ledge.

Women always pass first through doorways or even narrow passages on the street. It's a given. There is always a ready and willing man to be my companion to ensure I arrive safely at my destination, no matter how far it may be and no matter what time of the day or night.

I have grown to love being looked after in this way. For me it is new. I come from a culture where women have been conditioned to be overly masculine and to scoff when a man lends his hand; a culture where women are now reversing the roles and behaving with men in ways that are very unfeminine, aggressive and dominating.

More and more it seems women are not appreciative or acknowledging of the care and gifts men want to offer us. Emotional and mental abuse towards men from women is becoming more common as women gain more financial and economic power. The impact is actually quite demoralizing for the good men out there who truly want to be providers, givers and protectors.

I often question if the feminine empowerment movement has gone too far. Extreme feminism, as it is often demonstrated, actually offers insult to the natural balanced beauty of both the masculine and the feminine.

There is a natural order to our gender roles. When both sides are allowed to be in alignment with the natural order of life, harmony truly can exist. When one becomes over-dominating or oppressive, of course we enter into dysfunction and turmoil, and balancing out is needed. Yet it seems humans always have to take things to extreme.

The pendulum must swing as far to the right as it has to the left. Generations suffer before we can come back into balance and be at peace again. For many centuries, matriarchy dominated many parts of the world. In pre-Christian times, in many cultures, men were oppressed. Now we are living predominately in a patriarchal era. Women are again fighting for their rights and freedoms. Traditional roles, with clearly marked rites of passages and clear gender identifications are being lost, devalued and undermined. The porn industry is normalizing perversions that often stem from trauma and deep psychosis. Gender confusion is growing as experimental modifications that are not natural to our biology are being sold as the cure, and for enormous sums of money. The bigger picture of nature's inherent design is being invalidated completely.

In all truth, I much prefer being treated in this more traditional way. It feels more natural to me. It allows me to soften into a part of myself that I have been denied access to for most of my life as a woman in the United States. American men, for the most part, have forgotten how to treat a woman like a woman. It's not even their fault. They have been educated right out of it by over-vigilant feminists who take offense when a man opens a door or pulls out a chair for her in an effort to treat her well. The societal trend now leans towards overly sexualizing the female form and empowering women to be dominating and assertive, even aggressive. With so many women playing right along with the exact stereotype they claim that they don't want to be categorized under, the confusion thickens.

All of this has had a huge impact on issues between men and women. Women are putting on the face of extreme independence and overtly sexual demonstrations in clothing (or the lack of it), in the modern world. This leaves little space for men to show up in the ways that give them their masculinity and purpose in the context of a relationship with a woman. Men are givers, protectors and providers by nature. When we deny them those

attributes, we deny them their higher sense of manhood in many ways.

Modern women (myself included) have, in my eyes, become too fiercely independent and driven. Rather than feeling cherished and cared for when a man offers a hand, or defends her in some way, they assume it means men think them too weak or frail. I don't at all find that to be true of men when I speak with them about what drives them to protect and cherish women.

This defensive way of being doesn't really invite or allow men to be giving, nurturing, protective or chivalrous, even when their motives are pure and beautiful. It seems to me that men are not sure just how to be, act and treat women anymore in the modern world. Many men have shared with me that they find it really challenging to try to figure out how they should act, and be with women in the modern era. The over masculinization of the feminine has effectively emasculated the masculine and everyone is all mixed up on the gender roles as a result. If women continue to live in the story that they do not want or need men to care for them, protect, serve or assist them in any way, then what role does a man have left to play? If women continue to demonstrate this effectual castration of sorts, naturally, men will eventually stop caring or trying. Men need to feel appreciated and respected just as much as women do. Modern culture has created quite a vicious and confused mess out of the dance between man and woman.

In Cuba, remnants of traditional gender roles and values are still thriving. There is a deeper understanding between men and women of what is expected from each other. Gender roles are clearly defined. Men are celebrated as men, and allowed to be manly, and women are celebrated as women and allowed to be feminine. There is a powerful presence in both genders that can not be denied.

For that reason, Guaguanco is one of my favorite musical expressions on the island. It is a courtship dance that demonstrates the attraction of the masculine to the feminine, her

acknowledgment of his desire, and the sensual sweet play of a man and a woman exploring their attraction together. She invites him through flirtatious looks, hip swirls, shoulder shimmys, booty shakes and smiles. He uses his skills of coercion, with dignity and respect, combined with as much charm as he has in order to win her affection. It is a perfect example of what modern culture has robbed so many men and women of in today's world.

This alluring dance of passion requires the man and the woman both to appreciate and acknowledge each other's strengths and vulnerabilities equally. The inherent nature of the dance is sexy, fun, playful and tender. It always leaves me touched, and inspired.

My experience in my own culture is that dance may be one of the only strongholds we have left for exploring sensuality between each other in a safe and playful way. Sadly, I see that even in the dance, much of that is becoming lost in our world. Nightclubs and social dances are some of the only opportunities available, and typically people have to drink a lot of alcohol to get to a place where they can move their bodies and invite playfulness or sensuality in.

In most of these environments, there is very little of the kind of innocent playfulness that is so prevalent and commonplace amongst Cubans, even within their families. Too often in our modern, gender confused world, sexual crimes and horrible acts of violence happen from what started as playful, sensual explorations on the dance floor. The incredibly graphic overexposure that today's online live pornography has created has not only de-sanctified and demystified sex, and sexual attraction; it has created and empowered a new breed of sexual sickness that is running rampant through our world, affecting both men and women of all ages in all countries.

Perhaps another thing that has supported Cuba to still have some semblance of sexual purity and innocence is that pornography has been illegal on the island since Castro came in to power. Internet porn sites are strictly controlled and banned

in Cuba. Of course, this is not to say it doesn't exist in Cuba. However, it is not nearly as accessible, on a day to day basis, as it is in the rest of the world. People can google just about any sexually deviant behavior, including violent sexuality, and be exposed to things that are aberrations and dysfunctional sexual illnesses far removed from healthy normal sexuality or sacred union.

It seems to me that the tender, old fashioned way of courtship has been mostly lost in modern culture. The old ways of getting to know someone by spending quality time together have been traded for online dating, man or woman shopping online, and even "sex on demand hook up" sites. I feel so grateful that I grew up in the pre-internet era, and that I can remember the mystery of romance.

Perhaps that is another reason why I feel so much more comfortable and at home here in Cuba. The values here and the ways of being together are so much more in alignment with my own values on so many levels.

What I am witnessing in the United States, in the maddening race of better, faster, more, with technology, gender confusion, and sexual sicknesses, just does not match the imprint of my deeper awareness. It simply doesn't ring true to me. It is not any part of my soul's calling, not as a human being, and most certainly not as a woman.

Callejon de Hamel: Rhumba

I *am surprised today* by the moments of extreme emotion surging through me. Flashes of the past I am leaving behind dance behind my eyes. I find my attention distracted from the present as my future comes flying towards me. Unfortunately, too soon, I will be on a silver bird flying back across the ocean, leaving this musical paradise behind. I feel like a 10 year old who doesn't want to leave home being torn from her mama.

I am grateful that Ishmael will be here to escort me to Havana today. I know that he will miss me as much as I will miss him. For weeks, we have spent several hours a day together laughing, walking and sharing a natural and comfortable love and friendship, that is free of all but respect for each other. We are going today to Havana to the infamous Callejon de Hamel for the Sunday afternoon Rhumba to share our love of his culture with each other.

The alley is brightly painted with images of the Afro-Cuban Pantheon. Packed wall to wall with a jambalaya of Cubans and a few tourists, the music calls to all of us to escape the thoughts of the day and join in celebration through rhythmical ecstasy.

Here we enter a world where music is the master. There is an unspoken agreement that hangs like a thick veil in the air. We

all agree to serve the music's demands. The drums are furiously invoking the Orishas with incantations and powerful pulses of hands on skin, metal on metal, wood on wood. Hundreds of feet are pounding the earth in perfect timing to the drums. Voices are piercing the air as calls of the spirit world drift through the intricate rhythmical interplays. Everyone is singing and dancing; praying to the Orishas: the Gods and Goddesses of Santeria. I am entranced and fully captivated. All of me is drawn into the depths of the music. I surrender to it immediately. I am drawn into the heart of the magic. A strong black hand reaches out for mine and pulls me into the empty space in front of the drummers to watch and be shielded. Ishmael stands guard, protecting me from the sea of bodies behind me.

My body knows the rhythms well. I dance, sing and witness the magic, feeling the passionate energy of the performers, mixing with the cacophony of the crowd, driving the energy into a full-blown frenzy. I have no fear here. Ishmael warned me many times, "Ten cuidado con tus cosas aquf, a veces puede ser peligroso." Yet, I feel totally safe here. I actually feel protected surrounded by black bodies, singing hearts and wild furious rhythms. I close my eyes and journey into the spirit world, knowing I am in good company with others who understand trance and its healing effects.

Opening my eyes again, I take a quick visual inventory of the world around me. A blind boy sits next to me. I wonder what his experience is like. His small, soft hand occasionally reaches out and touches mine. Perhaps this is his way of finding a reminder that he is still close to others. I touch his hand reassuringly any time he reaches out. I am moved by the kinship we are sharing as complete strangers living in vastly different worlds.

I see a tall man with his eyes rolling back, the lids flickering, exposing the whites of his eyes as his trance deepens. He stands firmly planted in his experience, dressed in all white. Chaos is splashing about in the periphery with loud raucous voices of men who have had too many bottles of rum and not enough women

to satisfy their voracious appetites for passion. I love it. I am totally blissed out.

This goes on for hours. The hot sun shows no mercy to us. Everyone is sweating, dripping, and soaking wet. We have become a family of a special kind through sharing the songs and the day. A family of spirit, moving and praying together. The laughter is free, and plastic cups and bottles of rum are passed around freely. Several different groups of musicians have come in and out throughout the day, each group seeming to have the intention of taking it to the next level. Each group pushing the energy higher.

The ones that impressed me the most were the female Bata players. A rarity in Cuba, these women demonstrate a defiance to the old-world beliefs that women should not touch the sacred Bata. They stand for the breaking of an old tradition. I resonate, as this has been a familiar path for me. In that they have my ultimate respect.

The lead drummer and singer is a round boisterous black woman, her head wrapped in white fabric; her white clothes hanging down to the ground as she plays with a ferocity I know well. She is given some respect by her male counterparts but I can't help but notice how the male players jump in often and try to take over. She anchors it down and while she is forced to allowing some of it, rather than make a big scene, she stays powerfully anchored on her instrument through it all, never wavering for a moment, driving the energy to new levels. The challenges she has as a female Bata master are clearly written on her brow, and in her eyes. I feel the burn deep inside of me, as I witness her in her struggle as a woman playing a drum.

Women daring to go where few women ever have gone before is a surprising gift for me to see today. I can't help but reflect on my own challenges as a female percussionist, as I watch these women play and stand up to the challenge of the men. The memories bring tears to my eyes. I feel a tiny bit of protective

rage along with the tears, witnessing the disrespect these Queens of rhythm are managing during their set.

I recall the many nights playing in ceremony in the United States when men would come and try to dominate or challenge me in some weird unconscious way. It was evident that they were both afraid and in awe of the power of an empowered woman of the drum who lives in the domain of rhythm. I remember that feeling of disrespect all too well.

I feel the memory of the intensity of energy that could come through me in defiance of that kind of domination. I still remember well the bittersweet taste of those moments when the rage inside came out full force in resistance to the disrespect. There was power like I'd never known in that defiant rage. It took me many years to learn to temper that steel to be more compassionate and loving towards my brothers. "Forgive them for they know not what they do," became my mantra of healing.

I also remember the tears and the frustrations of not wanting to have to play the game their way. I spent too many nights challenged by the egotistical male dominated drumming community and the overbearingness of "louder, faster." Eventually I learned that I had to create my own way. I had to create a way to relax more into my feminine sensuality with the drum. I eventually learned how to be supported in playing soft, fast and with incredible precision and power, without having to be loud, fast and competitive all the time.

The blessing was creating whole new dimensions of rhythm, and grace out of those challenges. I remember the night that the Orishas first spoke to me through the rhythms. I remember how my spirit left my body and hovered in the other worlds, and the clear distinct message that was given to me that night. It was that message through the wind so many years ago that ultimately has me here now in Cuba.

Ishmael's voice calls to me from behind. He is guiding me out of the crowd, which has become totally out of control. He stays close to me to protect me from pickpockets and grabbers,

who might want to get a quick feel of an Americana in the packed crowd. With one hand on my shoulder, he towers over me, directing me out of the crowd with skillful agility as we move through the hundreds of sweating bodies. He is all business; a force of stability and safety for me after hours of singing, dancing and prayer. I am grateful for his strong, anchored presence. I had not realized, being in the center, the wildness that was going on behind me. The crowd is mostly drunk and the energy is totally intoxicating.

I smile up at Ishmael, in obvious enjoyment of the chaos and spirit of the day. He laughs heartily, "Aye Cheri, tu eres Cubana."

On our way back to Cojimar, Ishmael and I discuss some of the distinctions between my culture and Cuba, and the ways that Cuba will likely change once it is opened up more. I know that it is an inevitability. The innocence and magic here will undeniably be washed over with the plastic wrapped, shiny gloss emptiness of modern culture's influence. We both feel lucky to have experienced Cuba the way it is now, without McDonald's, computers and cell phones everywhere. Without the constant distractions from each other and what really matters.

Ishmael has a profound understanding of how his culture will be impacted by American culture. As a man who's lived through the Revolution, he is not one who wants to see too much change in Cuba. He is happy here as it is. Ishmael fears the day when Cuba becomes another territory for capitalism. Quite frankly, so do I.

Cuba has already been impacted, of course, by modern culture's influence. However, the traditions and culture here are still thriving and rich with mystery. Many people in the evenings are still talking on their front porches and spending time with friends, neighbors and family. The glow of TV can be seen from some homes, but still not all of them. It is easiest to see the fascination of modern mainstream culture in the youth. With their gold teeth, bling and pants hanging down to their knees

they are anxious to copy parts of popular United States culture without even understanding its origins or the meanings of things.

Many people here want change. Surprisingly, many people do not think it will ever change. Many have completely resigned themselves to total acceptance of Cuba always being as it is. My own personal perspective is not so important here, yet I find myself wanting change to come accompanied with a new mindfulness and awareness that has never been seen before. It is my prayer that Pandora's Box can be managed, and carefully deliberated.

The influence of the United States, mainstream culture and modern values (or lack of them) on tradition and culture has been devastating in most places of the world. Modern mainstream culture has been highly successful at robbing people of their own identity and devaluing their rich Ancestoral heritage. It is a well-known atrocity that we have seen too many times on the planet where the intangible aspects of a culture, their music, art, and organic ways of being together are undermined and devalued. It hurts my heart to consider this happening in Cuba.

I do not know what I can do to help, or if I can at all. I only know that I want to be a voice for the invitation of a wise and gentle transition that honors the culture and lifestyle here for what it is. My prayer is that if, and when, Cuba becomes a more open world, that it does not seek to replace what is sacred and valuable of Cuban culture, for what is cheap and commercial.

There is a billboard on the highway between Havana and Cojimar that boasts the promise of computers in every home, for every family. It makes me cringe every time I pass by it. I remember the days before computers and cell phones as some of the best times of my life. I remember the family sitting together for meals and talking about our day. I remember playing outside in nature with other boys and girls in the neighborhood. I remember what now almost seem like "the good old days," when no one could reach me if I was out of the house. There was still a sense of mystery and freedom in the world.

Statistics show higher rates of depression and mental disease than ever before in modern culture, but yet supposedly we are "more connected." How is it that being more connected has torn us from our families, communities and loved ones, and created such an immense loneliness in our hearts and minds?

I have been in Cuba now for almost 3 weeks without a computer. It has been one of the greatest gifts I could have ever given myself. I am not at all excited about returning to spending hours in front of an EMF-producing machine that gives me headaches, takes me away from the present reality, distracts my mind, and keeps me occupied with bullshit that I really do not care so much about. I would be quite happy to return to a life without emails and Facebook. All of it can go with no regrets on my part. I would happily give it up in a minute. I imagine someday, that I will. I certainly intend to.

Returning to Cojimar, I feel a sense of sad sweetness arising between Ishmael and myself. We both know this is the last night we will walk the streets of this little village, laughing and sharing our lives together. As if on cue, the wind picks up and whispers through my hair softly. It is a gentle reminder that she will never leave me. Even when I leave this rock that I have come to love more than my own land, she will remain with me as my messenger and ally.

Ishmael looks at me as the wind picks up and smiles knowingly. I reach for his arm, threading mine through his. We walk in silence back to my casa. We are pure companions in life, friends, brother and sister, *familia*. I know he will come tomorrow to see me off before I leave. Neither of us has the heart to address the reality of my departure right now. It will not be easy for either of us.

Neither of us wants tomorrow to come.

The Return

Oya's breath is suspended like my heart in time. She is quiet and the sea is calm. The sky is heavy and promising of a storm. There has not been one since I arrived, but surely today it is coming. I am sad that I will miss it.

I love storms. I am the most alive when the skies are opening and lightning is crackling thru the air. I want nothing more than to stay here in the midst of this growing storm and be embraced by it.

Slowly, the waves roll beneath the surface in gentle soft undulations of time passing. I sit watching them, hypnotized by their perfect sweet groove. I can see why 6/8 is the most common musical time signature here. The ocean rolls in it, round and fluid like a big woman's hips dancing rhumba. It feels as if the wind is bidding me farewell by letting the seas be so calm. She has barely stopped blowing since I arrived. This is by far the calmest I've seen the ocean in three weeks. Is she mourning my departure too? The metaphor of the calm before the storm does not escape me.

I don't want to go. I've never not wanted to go so badly. I think I am dying today. My head aches and it feels like acid is moving through my veins, not blood. Everything inside and out hurts. Sitting up makes me almost pass out. It is my last day here. As I hobble painstakingly to the toilet, I marvel that in 20 days here this is the first time I have had any real stomach issues. It is

not, however, the first time I have felt like death on this journey. A rerun of an incident I had a few weeks ago tells me my timing to leave may be perfect, in spite of my resistance.

A week ago, with Ishmael in Pinar del Rio, I felt some similar stirrings in my little body. An incredible headache and acute, stabbing pain on the right side of my abdomen. The feeling of acid in my veins does not make for good company. A double visit of this pain is something to pay attention to for me. Last week, I thought maybe I had just fought off the flu, it was so quick. While intense, I did not have any vomiting or major stomach trouble. To have a return of those symptoms along with vomiting and intense nausea, is most certainly cause for concern.

For four hours, I lie in bed hovering between what feels like life and death. I am quite peaceful despite the pain. I let my mind wander and find it entertaining a bizarre, yet somehow peaceful fantasy of what it would be like to die here today in Cuba. The pain is so intense that at present, it's almost a comforting possibility.

I have had a great life. I have lived a life most people only dream of. My life has been so full of beauty, magic, love and goodness, with just the right amount of challenge, struggle and heartbreak, to make me a wizened aged one already. Death is not really so scary for me. Being in this much physical pain, knowing I have to return to a world where I just do not really fit in at all, makes death almost welcome today.

I have lived as an authentic being, real and honest with my reality. When I am happy, I am happy. When things take a turn for the worse, I let it take a turn for the worse. I find my way through it all day by day. I have lived and walked this life in my own way, mostly by my own design, and as a wild and wise woman. I have never been one to try to please others just to gain acceptance or social standing, and I have never been able to be something or someone I am not. If then, that is my sole accomplishment in this life, I can ie here today in peace.

I hear Ishmael's voice, cheerful and boisterous, talking to Barbarita outside. I know that I need to gather my strength to sit up, finish packing, dress and get ready for my taxi to the airport. I remember that a sweet young woman from England gave me some Ibuprofen and pain killers somewhere along the journey. I scramble through my bag to find them, pop them in my mouth and pray they will digest before I vomit again.

When I see Ishmael's big beautiful smile, it lifts my spirits and gives me courage to face my emerging reality. I realize how much I will miss this man who has become such a good friend to me in such a short time. He has been a rock for me here. Even though it has only been three weeks, I know our friendship will last forever. Ishmael visits with me for a little while. When he leaves I have to fight like crazy to hold back the tears. We embrace three times, both knowing the other has been transformed through our friendship. Both also knowing that we will most definitely see each other again and that our lives will be forever intertwined in this world and the worlds beyond.

A few nights ago, he asked me to accompany him to the river before he walked me home. He carried a plastic bag with a big squash in it. I thought maybe he was selling it or gifting it to a friend. We walked under the moon appreciating the night together. As we passed stinking piles of trash in the streets that flowed all the way into the sea, we began to talk of the gravity of the problem of waste management in Cuba.

The people don't seem to take much notice or care, but the ocean's edges (and really all of town), are overflowing with garbage. After speaking with a few Cubans I realized that they do care, but no one really knows what to do about it or how to deal with the growing problem of waste management here. Children play barefooted and bare-bottomed in the rocky tide pools near the ocean. In these pools there are huge shards of glass and broken metal jutting out in the rocks, hiding in almost every crevice, nook and cranny. The government does provide some

trash collection services, but the issue is greater than what the resources to manage it provide for.

Ishmael and I agree that this is one thing that the influence of modern culture could be beneficial for. This could specifically mean providing help to clean up the messes by providing infrastructure, training and resources that are sorely needed here. However, it seems to me that one of the most powerful ways we could contribute would be in offering educational programs and initiatives to raise awareness about waste management, recycling and waste reduction. Considering the fact that modern culture brings with it whole new issues of waste with hundreds of tons of plastics and other newly introduced environmental toxins, it seems to me that it should be a built-in component wherever our greedy little paws touch foreign soil.

The moon shimmers across the river as a fishing boat heads out to sea. A beautiful vision is cast before my eyes that I will always hold dear in my memory: a starry sky, softly waving palms, a few flickering lights of the village across the bay, soft rhythms fading in and out of the breeze, and one lone fisherman heading out to sea beneath a silver globe that cascades its light into the darkness. The magic of the moment does not escape me. I sip it in, savoring it in my consciousness, like I would savor a fine red wine or delicious truffle.

We cross over the rickety bridge to the river's edge. The squash is an offering to his Orisha, *Oshun*. Oshun is the Yoruban deity that presides over the rivers and fresh waters. She is the essence of playful, flirtacious sensuality. She represents luxury, pleasure, sexuality, fertility, beauty and love. She is connected to destiny and divination. She has immense power over men. She can draw them in with her beauty to do her will with a coy detachment that somehow hooks them even deeper than her overpowering sensuality. All men desire her love and affection. She dresses in yellow and dances with a provocative smile that comes from the pleasure she gives to herself. She enjoys her body

and her life fully, with unreserved freedom. She is the primary consort of the male Orisha known as *Chango* (aka Shango).

Chango is known for his promiscuity. Being a bit of a lady's man, he also took Oya for his consort amongst others. He is known to be the god of lightning, thunder, fire, war, Bata drums, dance, music and masculine beauty. He is the patron of warriors and a force to be reckoned with. He can be argumentative and easily angered and, as such, the color he is represented by is a fiery red. Chango is also known to be loyal and hardworking. He is a dedicated ally. It was the altar of Chango that I saw the first day when I visited Ishmael's home. Feeling connection with me as a lover of *Oya*, it all makes perfect sense to me.

I am touched that he would invite me to witness his offering to Oshun. He places the squash by the river quite unceremoniously. We walk back to my place quietly together. I am giggling inside, seeing what a simple easy ritual it is.

I think of all the self-proclaimed shamans and priestesses in the New Age community of the United States who I have been exposed to along my journey. Many would likely go to great lengths to make this simple, daily practice some kind of an overly-dramatized, high-priced experience, rather than appreciating the simple, organic integration that this is for a Santero in Cuba.

There is no fluff or superfluous stuff in a Santeria Ceremony. It is so simple, pure, and organic in the way it is practiced in Cuba. Making an offering to his Orisha does not mean he has to close his eyes, hold his hands to the air and make a proclamation of some sort. It is the most unceremonious of ceremonies on the outside, because it is so clearly practiced and understood on the inside.

He has no need or desire to draw even the slightest amount of attention to himself. It is just a quiet contemplative stroll to the riverside. A laying down of a squash without the utterance of even a word. The action itself is the prayer and offering. Ceremony here is not some big episode to get all proper and

pompous about. I have found that to be the case in many other countries religious ceremonies as well.

Before we reach my casita, I stop with him under the moonlight and look at him. This beautiful human being who stands before me has touched and transformed my life in three weeks in ways that will be ever unfolding. He has become one of my best friends of all times.

"I will miss you deeply. Thank you for everything Ishmael." I said to him. He puts his huge arm around me and says nothing, but smiles gently.

We walked arm in arm for a few strides before he said in Spanish, "Es el amor lo que importa Cheri." (It's love that matters.) I knew that he would miss me too, this gentle loving giant of a man. As we walked the remaining few blocks back to my place, I let the tears stream down my face freely, knowing I was held by an angel.

Getting back to Costa Rica is barely a welcome relief. At best, it is a better first stop than going direct to the United States, which feels like it would be traumatic culture shock. I have always found that I experience culture shock much more when I return to my own country, than when I leave it. The blaring lights and indifference of the people, combined with the neurotic frenzied rush-rush-rush pace of life instantly impact me. It often leaves me a bit confused at how I ended up incarnating in a country that feels mostly like it's at war with, and direly opposed to, my humanity.

I ask the taxi driver to stop so I can buy a bag of fruit to calm my acidic stomach which is still burning inside with ferocity. I will spend the evening at one of my favorite guest houses in San Jose, with Eduardo, who runs the place. I met Eduardo three years ago when I was traveling through San Jose and stayed at his guest house. He is a lovely, articulate and handsome man. It is a warm, familiar place to stop and rest before heading back to chilly Denver.

We stay up late drinking wine and chatting about the social problems in Cuba, Costa Rica and the United States. When I get up to go to my room, he catches me off guard and kisses me full on the lips. I can feel his desire simmering below the surface and I am only a little bit surprised. I am just not interested, even as handsome and lovely as he is. I smile, push him back, and politely but firmly say goodnight. He gently clings to me, then lets my arm and hand roll through his hand, an obvious test to see if I will linger or be seduced back in. I do not linger. I am not tempted. Luckily, he is a gentleman and I am able to go to sleep in peace. I just do not have the heart for playing with a man yet in any way. My heart is in Cuba. I am devoted fully to loving myself.

I go to sleep, with a little smile in my heart. I can feel his desire lingering in the room on the other side of the wall. I remember to thank God that I did not die in Cuba and give thanks that the pain in my body is finally starting to subside. In a few hours, I will be back in the good old United States of America. Overall, I feel as ready as I can be, although perhaps simply surrendered to the reality of what must be is a more truthful confession.

I left my country almost three months ago feeling very alone, scared and insecure, wondering if I was indeed going crazy. I was doing everything possible to avoid seeing my reflection in the mirror for more than the briefest of moments. I would look as quickly as possible just to make sure that my face had not fallen into the abyss that the rest of me seemed to be barely existing in.

I felt unspeakably unattractive, even almost invisible. I felt more like a hollow shell than the joyful spirited woman I once remembered myself as. I had been defeated. My ego was fully deflated, bruised and burnt to a crisp. An eight-year relationship that I had devoted my heart, body, mind and soul to had left me feeling abandoned, degraded and a lot like chopped liver. My self-esteem was struggling to feel worthy of even getting out of bed. I truly was a sad shadow of the woman I had once been.

I do not think many people could see it from the outside, or at least no one seemed to notice, but inside I was a wasteland. Looking in the mirror was too hard because when I did, I saw the saddest, angriest and most distraught little lady I could never have imagined myself to be. I was broken. My trust in men, but more so in love, was shattered completely by lies and deception. I felt so deeply betrayed by love, by the man who I had loved, and by life itself. Prior to that I truly believed that love alone was enough to conquer anything. Suddenly, I found myself looking down the barrel of a whole different reality. Everything I had believed in was revealed to me as lies and illusion.

I am returning now to my country in joyful reclamation of the powerful strong woman that I know I truly am. I am humbled by the journey. I can see that the downturn has only served to make me more human, and more in touch with my core essence as a woman, and human being. I am confident again in my ability to find and be love in a myriad of forms, people, expressions, cultures and most importantly, within myself.

I do not need my sense of well-being and love to come from a man. A relationship does not define me, nor does it need to define my experience of life and reality. With or without a partner, I can enjoy each and every moment of my existence loving fully and receiving life fully. I am passionately in love again with my own sensuality as a woman. I know that I live to love as the wind does, without need or attachment. I aim to fly freely and to be as expressed, joyful and wild as I feel, whenever I feel. I know that I have the inner compass of wisdom to guide me and keep me safely in the company of angels and kind souls.

I know again that the more that I am just who and what I am, the more love is awaiting me. I have no idea how I am going to survive now. I do not yet know how I will find enough money to keep going. More importantly, the burning question is how and when will I get myself back to Cuba. I can't know now how the next pieces will unfold.

What I do know is that I am now comfortable and completely OK with all of it. I now have the confidence in myself to know that I will be OK no matter what. I know also that no man can give me what I need to be a completely expressed woman in the ways that I love being. I must claim that for myself, and then possibly one day, when, or if, the right man finds me, I can share myself with him from that place of empowered self-awareness. I can dance in fearlessly authentic self-expression.

I will accept nothing less.

I am returning as the Phoenix rising from the ashes of her own destruction. I am once again willing to step into this beautiful play of life as a master of the moment. My heart is bejeweled and crowned by my own love for myself. My hands are ready to play with new passion, purpose and power. I am walking into this new life, naked to my core, but well adorned with the essence of an authentic awakened wild and wise woman.

The Breath of Cuba

Part 2

Chapter 1

Two Years Later...

Returning to the Rock

The tires of the plane hit the ground and the plane erupts into a joyous yip. Already the expressive spirit of this island is singing through me. We have arrived in Cuba. I feel a ridiculously delicious sense of coming home. It feels warm and welcoming, and just slightly tinged with the elusive intriguing sense of despair that I know is also deep in the heart of Cuba and its people.

My Cuban lover sits next to me. He touches my hand lightly and smiles. I want to devour him right now and pray that tonight we can be together. It has been more than two weeks now since we have been able to enjoy each other.

I am excited for the moment when I can pull him close to me to incite his incantations of primal passion and pleasure. I have been trying to tell myself I will not sleep with him again, but the draw is so strong, we both know it's inevitable. I want him and I am not going to deny myself the pleasure, not now, not in Cuba. Not after all we've both gone through to be here together.

I also know that getting through customs will be a game of hoop jumping and tolerance, of trying to smile even as the contents of my bag are spread out and ripped through by customs officers. I wonder if travelling with a Cuban and his family will make it easier or more difficult for me.

The airport looks bleak and uninviting, almost intimidating. There is a soft haze spreading across the tarmac. I know that

beyond that stagnant illusion lies a world of magic, music and men awaiting me, and for that I am excited. It has been almost two years since I was here last. There is so much that has changed, both on this island and especially within me.

I smile inwardly reflecting on the growth that has come in two years of being single. My lover's strong black hand grasps my thigh with ardor as I lay my head back against the seat. His passion burns right into me. My body softens and tingles in anticipation for his lips on my skin. He is my first Cuban lover and I am quite sure that he won't be my last.

Closing my eyes briefly. I reflect on the movie of memories in my mind of the last trip. I was so shut down to men, intimacy or any kind of romantic connection when I was in Cuba last time. Yet, I remember the sensations that were roused here all too well. The intoxicating passion and desire that the men stirred in me just passing them on the streets as they looked through me. The heat their eyes could well up from inside of me, despite my walls and defenses. I am most definitely a very different woman now than I was then. I find myself excited by new possibilities and silently giggle in lustful delight.

In the past two years, I have shed layer after layer of my conditioning, fears, insecurities and social pretenses. I have uncovered the essence of the wild woman within me as much as the wise one. It has been a journey of ripping away the soul suffocating stories that my culture taught me of how a woman should behave to be respectable, proper and socially accepted.

I have found peace with my emotional, raving, bitch self as much as my rational, clear, soft and sensual aspects. I have delved deep into the sensual stirrings of my femininity and granted them full permission to find enjoyment in men, who I once would have been afraid to consider because of the social and cultural stigmas I once learned. I stomped out the prude in me and claimed my huntress as an active and titillating part of my being. I faced her with eyes wide open, peering steadfast into the darkness, pleasure and wisdom that she can invite.

I found that at 40 years old, there was an insatiable sexual hunger burning in me that I had never felt. I found pleasure in the lip licking lust that it birthed in me. I grew to understand the younger man's fascination with the mature woman, and vice versa. I found a somewhat disgusted, but profound understanding in the term cougar (as much as I hated the word and its connotations) when I found myself prowling the night alone, contemplating the deeper worlds of my own inner sexuality in quiet observation of the thoughts and impulses that were flowing through me.

I felt the big cat within me and embraced her wholeheartedly, setting her free on occasion to hunt, feast and enjoy. I learned that my feline intuitive wisdom as a woman also blesses me with clear discernment on which men to steer clear of, and which ones are safe. I relearned that dancing enables me to enjoy the chase without always needing to feast on the catch so that my temple and mind can remain safe and clear.

I discovered that I had been hiding certain parts of myself out of a fear of the power of their expression and I kicked that shit to the curb. My inhibitions and stories about what was "ok" for me as a woman were crushed by the overpowering need to be real with what I was feeling, and to find the truth of myself on all levels. I let myself feel, react, respond and be authentic in my expressions in every way. The result is that I have found infinite grace pouring through me in every moment that is mine to claim.

I jumped into full acceptance of being and loving myself exactly as I am with no holds barred. There are no more resistances to my true feelings. I stood naked with myself and hurled a stone of intent at the mirrors of my mind's conditioning. I let all the illusions shatter. I found myself standing fearlessly in the unveiling of both the wild and the wise within me, as the shards fell to the ground in a cacophony of simultaneous destruction and creation.

I have spent the past two years experimenting with new paradigms for relationships without such heavy emotional

investments. Most importantly perhaps, I committed that I would never again lose myself in the arms and illusions of a man's love. I decided that being single offered me tremendous freedom and opportunity. It allows me to create my life on my own terms, and to live my dreams fully. I committed that I would not compromise what I want in a relationship just to be with someone, no matter how wonderful the sex or the love is.

I came to terms with the reality that sometimes, just for pure fun, I welcome bad boys with bulging biceps and rock hard bodies that just want some hot steamy passion with no strings attached. I learned be fully alive.

I discovered that there is actually something incredibly liberating about two adults with no drama, no stories, and no emotional baggage giving themselves fully to each other for a night or many nights of pleasure and adult play.

I have faced loneliness, depression and my own deep fears of unworthiness, and accepted that they are companions, I will walk this life with forever. I befriended them as my allies to deeper understandings. I no longer fear the run from them. As Ram Daas once said of his neurosis, "I invite them in for tea."

In short, I got real with myself and found that I can love and accept all of it if I stop resisting what simply is. I redefined what it means to be a liberated, empowered woman at middle age, and I feel sexier, more alive and happier than I ever have. I am free to be me, fully, totally, authentically myself and that for me is peace.

His soft full lips brush my ear and I feel my sexy loverr"s hot breath whispering to me. Instantly, my body stirs in response to him.

"Baby, te quiero, no puedo esperar para ti." His tongue curls perfectly around my ear. I want only him. I say nothing and simply smile.

"Vamos," he says and we are in motion, grabbing bags and filing off the plane.

He slaps my ass lightly on the way out. I feel a pleasant jolt of desire stir within me. I am smiling in joyous delight as we

walk onto the tarmac and Cuba's hot steamy stinky air greets my senses.

The Breath of Cuba stirs in me again.

For More Excerpts and Video Footage of the story

The Breath of Cuba

Visit Cheri online at
www.thebreathofcuba.com

Be sure to order your copy of Part II

cherishanti.com